£2.50

Talli

THE BRADT MINI GUIDE

Neil Taylor

Bradt Travel Guides Ltd, UK
The Globe Pequot Press Inc, USA

First published 2004

Bradt Travel Guides Ltd, 19 High Street, Chalfont St Peter, Bucks SL9 9QE, England
Published in the USA by The Globe Pequot Press Inc, 246 Goose Lane, PO Box 480,
Guilford, Connecticut 06437-0480

Text copyright © 2004 Neil Taylor
Maps copyright © 2004 Bradt Travel Guides Ltd

A catalogue record for this book is available from the British Library

ISBN 1 84162 096 3

Cover Viru Gate (Tricia Hayne)
Text photographs Hilary Bradt (HB), Tricia Hayne (TH), Jonathan Smith (JS)
Maps Steve Munns   *Illustrations* Carole Vincer

Typeset from the author's disc by Wakewing
Printed and bound in Spain by Grafo SA, Bilbao

Neil Taylor is Director of Regent Holidays, a British tour company that has specialised in travel to the Baltic states since they regained their independence in 1991. He visits Estonia about four times a year, notebook in hand, catching up with the constant changes and raiding all the bookshops to add to the enormous collection on Tallinn he already has. He also writes and broadcasts on travel-trade topics and teaches on tourism courses at a number of different universities. In 2000, he won the Lifetime Achievement Award from the British Guild of Travel Writers for his work in opening up the Communist world to tourism. Should he ever stop writing, he will finally have time to learn Estonian.

FEEDBACK REQUEST

It doesn't matter how often I visit Tallinn: every time I go there, there is something new to entice the visitor. If you would like to share your comments about places I have mentioned in the guide, or tell me about something new that you have discovered, please do drop me a line at neiltaylor90@hotmail.com, or c/o Bradt Travel Guides, 19 High Street, Chalfont St Peter, Bucks SL9 9QE.

Author

Baltic Holidays

Since starting out as Lithuanianholidays.com in 2000, we have branched out to become Baltic Holidays, a specialist tour operator to the Baltic States of Lithuania, Latvia & Estonia.

Specialists in:
- City breaks to Vilnius, Riga & Tallinn
- Baltic Tours and country tours
- Tailor-made travel throughout the Baltics
- Family holidays
- City & Spa breaks
- City & Coast breaks
- Family research

Why use us ..?
- We are the only specialist UK travel company to deal solely with the Baltic States
- We visit Lithuania, Latvia & Estonia regularly
- Regular updates with our hotels and suppliers
- Up to date information on the best places to go
- We are fully ATOL bonded, ABTA bonded and members of AITO.

"Our travel through the Baltic States with your company went without a hitch and your wealth of local knowledge ensured we saw most of what there was to see and gain a rewarding insight to these wonderful countries."

Mr & Mrs South, tailor-made Baltic trip, May 03

Go with the leaders not the followers. You won't be disappointed.

Contact details:
Baltic Holidays, 40 Princess Street, Manchester M1 6DE
Tel: 0870 757 9233 Fax: 0870 120 2973
www.balticholidays.com Email: info@balticholidays.com

Contents

Contents

All foreign writers on Estonia begin their research at the Estonian Institute, either at their offices or via their website. Many go no further, such is the extent of the resources available from them. Guidebook writers do of course spend much time pounding the streets, but for anything not instantly available to the naked eye, or the many interpretations needed on what is seen, their help is always invaluable.

Acknowledgements

Whether approached by air, land or sea, Tallinn is immediately identifiable as a capital that looks west rather than east. The departure board at the airport lists London, Berlin, Copenhagen, Paris and Stockholm but rarely Minsk, Moscow or St Petersburg. The boats that fill the harbour, be they massive ferries or small yachts, head for Finland and Sweden, not Russia. The traffic jams that are beginning to block the main streets are caused by Volkswagens, Land Rovers and Saabs, not by Ladas. Links with the West are celebrated, such as the Eurovision Song Contest held in Tallinn in May 2002. Those with Russia are commemorated; flags are lowered every June 14 in memory of those deported to Siberia on that day in 1941. In 2002, Estonia joined NATO and on May 1 2004 it will join the EU. Its eastern borders become ever more tightly patrolled as they perhaps now represent the new Iron Curtain.

Immediately after independence Western goods started pouring into the shops and Russian ones are now very hard to find. There is a similar reluctance to buy from any of the other former Soviet republics. Travel agents offer the same tempting prices for holidays in Turkey, Greece and Italy that are available in western Europe, but nobody is interested in St Petersburg or the Crimea. Architecturally, with the exception of the Alexander Nevsky Cathedral which the last Tsarist regime bequeathed to Tallinn in the 1890s, it is the Germans, Swedes and Danes who have left their imposing mark on the churches and fortifications of the Old Town. Tallinn was often ready to defend itself but in the end never did so with fighting, which always took place in the outskirts and surrounding countryside and never in the city itself. This must to some extent be due to the city walls; when they were completed in the mid 16th century, after 200 years of building, they were over 2km long, nearly 3m thick and boasted 40 towers. Much of the wall remains today, as do 20 of the towers.

The nearest Tallinn came to a major battle was at the conclusion of the Northern War in 1710, but plague had reduced the population from 10,000 to 2,000 so the Swedes (who inhabited the city at the time) offered little resistance to the army of Peter the Great. It has suffered many occupations but, apart from a Soviet bombing raid in March 1944, the city has never been physically harmed.

Most tourists will be unaware of this 1944 raid as they wander in the Old Town along lanes built for horses and pedestrians rather than for cars. Restoration they will see everywhere, but new architecture is totally banned. They will need to cope with cobbles and steps and, where pavements exist at all, they will be uneven. A financial district is arising a good mile away where a building more than one hundred years old is as rare as a 20th-century one in the Old Town. With Estonia's only financial crisis now a distant memory from the early 1990s, most participants on the Tallinn stock market have seen nothing but constant gains. The building boom here reflects this. Only the trams link the two parts of town, although affluent young Estonians would never be seen dead on them. To them, public transport is only for the Russians left over from the Soviet occupation and for pensioners whose savings were all in worthless roubles.

The division in Tallinn between what is now the Old Town on the hill (Toompea) and the newer town around the port has survived political administrations of every hue. It has divided God from Mammon, Tsarist and Soviet governors from their reluctant Estonian subjects, and now the Estonian parliament from successful bankers, merchants and manufacturers who thrive on whatever coalition happens to be in power. Tallinn has no Capitol Hill or Whitehall. Government takes place between boutiques, embassies and the occasional residence. The parliament building is one of the most modest in the Old Town, dwarfed by the town walls and surrounding churches. When fully restored, the Old Town will be an outstanding permanent monument to Gothic architecture, and to a lesser extent to baroque as well. It will be a suitable backcloth to formal political and religious activity. Outside its formidable walls, contemporary Tallinn is changing rapidly according to the demands of the new business ethos. Concrete, slate and wood are giving way to glass and steel.

Introduction

Email addresses Where one is given, assume that correspondence in English is fine.

Hotel prices These always fluctuate wildly according to the booking agency used, the time of year and the day of the week. Take those listed only as a rough indication and, with the number of hotels due to open in Tallinn during 2004, expect some reductions.

Map references (eg: [2 G1]) relate to the colour map section at the end of the guide.

Opening hours Not many cafés open for breakfast as hotels include it in their room rates and Estonians live close enough to work to be able to eat at home before they leave. Once open from 10.00 or so, they divide into those which close around 17.00 and those likely still to be open at 24.00. Restaurants open at 12.00 and do not usually close during the afternoon. Their closing times vary enormously so if you want to eat late, you will certainly have a choice, but check the closing time if you have a particular favourite. Restaurants open seven days a week throughout the year and, much as they would like to pretend otherwise, bookings in advance are rarely necessary.

Most museums close at least one day a week, some for two days. Usually this is a Monday or Tuesday. They open around 10.30–11.00 and close around

17.00–18.00. Policies vary around national holidays so do check beforehand at those times. Pre-booked groups can usually arrange for museums to be opened specially for them.

Restaurant prices These always include VAT but rarely service; adding 10% for this is normal practice. Fixed price lunches are beginning to be offered but this is still not common in Tallinn and prices are usually the same for lunch and for dinner.

Websites In this book it can normally be assumed that if a website address is given, it has an English text. Many restaurants publish their menus on their sites.

How to use this book

TALLINN AT A GLANCE

Location Estonia is most northern of the Baltic states, bordering Latvia to south and Russia to north and east. Tallinn is on Gulf of Finland, 80km from Helsinki. Flights from London take about 3 hours, from Helsinki by helicopter about 20 minutes. Boats to Helsinki take 2–3 hours; bus to Riga about 5 hours

Population 380,000

Language Estonian

Religion Amongst the small number of Estonians who profess a religion, the Lutheran and Orthodox faiths predominate.

Time GMT/BST +2 hours (as neighbouring Baltic states)

International telephone code +372

Currency Estonian kroon (EEK), €1 = 15.65EEK

Electricity 220v; two-pin plugs

Public holidays January 1, February 24, June 23–24, August 20, December 25

School holidays Mid-June to mid-August, short breaks at Christmas and Easter

Climate Daytime temperatures November–February around 0°C, March–May, September–October, 10–20°C; June–August 20–25°C

HISTORY

Written records on Tallinn date only from the 12th century although it is clear that a small port existed well before then. In 1219 the Danes occupied Tallinn and much of what is now northern Estonia, on the pretext of spreading Christianity. The name Tallinn dates from this time and in Estonian actually means 'Danish city'. Although this name was chosen to suggest only temporary occupation, it has been maintained. The first German merchants settled in 1228 and they were to maintain their economic domination until 1939, even during the long periods of Swedish and Tsarist rule. Their elaborate coats of arms, displayed in the Dome and Niguliste churches, were a formal expression of this power. When, for instance, the Swedes surrendered to the Russians in 1710, the capitulation documents confirmed that German would remain the official language of commerce. Reval, the German name for Tallinn, is sometimes seen in English publications; it probably comes from *Revala*, the old Estonian name for the surrounding area. A more colourful explanation is that it comes from the two German words *Reh* and *Fall*, meaning the falling of the deer as they attempt to escape the Danish occupation.

Peter the Great visited Tallinn on 11 different occasions, so crucial was the city as an ice-free port to his empire. In 1711 he joined Christmas celebrations in Town Hall Square. He instigated the permanent expansion of Tallinn beyond the city walls by building Kadriorg Palace near the coast about two miles from the Old Town. The previous history of constant warfare at least in the vicinity of the town had led to all buildings being makeshift wooden houses which could easily be burnt as a

TALLINN BEFORE WORLD WAR II

From 'Keepers of the Baltic Gates' by John Gibbons, written in autumn 1938

Tallinn fascinated me; it is like plenty of other cities with an old part on top of a hill and a new part down below. If that was all I had wanted, I need have gone no further from London than Lincoln. But it was the general atmosphere and the people which so struck me. Here was none of the wealthy prosperity of Stockholm nor the studied modernity of Helsinki. Instead I was seeing a melange that I had met nowhere else with a ferocious grasp at gaiety that was as far removed from the natural happiness of Latindom as from the unbending stolidity of Saxonhood and Scandinavia.

On top of the Tallinn hill, I was in a quarter that might almost have been an English cathedral close. The nobility used to live there, but now it houses government ministries whose gentlemen staff might almost have been English themselves, so perfectly do they speak our tongue. Up and down all Estonia there are plenty of similar gentlemen politely eager to show their hospitality to the stranger and to make a guest welcome to their land.

preliminary defence to the city. Tallinn was then to enjoy 200 years of peace and increasing prosperity. Architecturally, though, the Old Town has always remained the centre of Tallinn and its main attraction. Gert Walter, a Baltic German who

Contexts

Coming downhill again, the streets were not the decorous promenades of cultured Finland. Here and there will be a chattering group of girls in what they think are the latest fashions of the Western world and then there could be a couple of old men in huge shabby coats that were probably first worn in Russian days now 20 years past. Everywhere there were students. In a land as new as prairie Canada one rather wonders how on earth they are going to find employment for all these anxious scholars.

By accident I found myself at what the guidebook calls the 'unimpressive Swedish Church of St Michael'. The architecture was indeed unimpressive – I only recall a lot of whitewash – but the congregation was the reverse. These people was so terribly and so whole-heartedly earnest. As the preacher droned on, even I of an alien creed could appreciate their attentiveness. There was no apparent oratory, no gestures, no ritual, nothing but the Word of God and they were following every word with an almost fierce eagerness. There is nothing indifferentist about Estonia.

settled in East Germany and could therefore return to Tallinn during the Soviet period, describes the Old Town as having half a per cent of the surface area of Tallinn but giving it its entire magic.

History

A DESCRIPTON OF TALLINN IN 1984
Kate Wharton

I spent last week in one of the saddest cities in the world, Tallinn in Estonia, famed for its medieval and 18th-century architecture. Extraordinarily, this tiny backwater of the Soviet Empire has been in the news recently as its people were warned by the voice of *Pravda*, Moscow's main daily newspaper at the time, that they were not Soviet enough. Suddenly the secrets of this benighted land began to emerge. So, last week, determined to find out about the real Estonia, I became the first Western journalist in the country for many, many months, and certainly the first since Estonia came back into the news.

At issue in Estonia is the enforced russification of their land and the disappearance of their language and all their customs. The blue, black and

The completion of the railway link with St Petersburg in 1870 turned Tallinn into a major city. The port was enlarged to handle the increasing volume of goods that could now be brought there and factories were established to take advantage of the larger markets. In the 20th century, most events that would determine Estonia's future took place in Tallinn. Independence was declared there in 1918 and in 1991, German occupations were imposed there also in 1918 and again in 1941. The

Contexts

white flag of independent Estonia was banished in 1944. Today the Russian flag is everywhere. So is the huge figure of 40, accompanied by a hammer and sickle, to remind everyone that the yoke has been in place for 40 years and is intended to be there in excess of 40 x 40. Already more than half the population, 52%, is Russian rather than Estonian and by 1987, when the vast military harbour outside Tallinn is finished, the proportion will rise to 65%.

About 65,000 Estonians fled to the West in 1944. Thousands more were deported to remote parts of the Soviet Union and most of the present-day dissidents now rot in Russian labour camps. As Ernst Jaakson, Estonian Consul-General in New York, told me: 'There is hardly an Estonian family in existence that has not been separated from its loved ones or nearest relatives as a result of the Soviet occupation.'

Published in 'The Mail on Sunday', September 2 1984

Soviets came in 1940 and then chased the Germans out in 1944. In the 20th century, the Russians and Germans between them occupied Tallinn seven times, and the country has been independent three times, although it has to be admitted that independence on the first occasion in 1918 lasted only for one day. Britain can claim considerable credit for ensuring that the next period of independence would last much longer – 20 years. Intervention by the Royal Navy during 1918–19 in the Gulf

History

of Finland near Tallinn ensured that neither the Bolsheviks nor the Germans were able to conquer Estonia at that time.

The port always adapted to the political circumstances in which it found itself. During the first independence period from 1920 to 1940 it exported large quantities of timber and dairy products to Britain as the market to the new Soviet Union was lost. Passenger services linked it with all its Baltic neighbours. It would suffer a moribund 45 years from 1945 until 1990 with little international trade being allowed. The twice-weekly ferry service that operated for Finnish visitors from the 1960s rapidly increased to a boat an hour during the 1990s as the notorious 'vodka tourists' poured in, together with some other visitors who had broader interests. Whilst 2.5 million passengers a year come to Tallinn on this route, the port has to battle hard with Russian, Latvian and Lithuanian ports for the transit traffic in goods from Russia and Central Asia.

Between 1945 and 1990 the city's population doubled in size to 500,000, about 30% of the total population of Estonia. Since then, Tallinn's population, like that of the whole country, has dropped considerably as women delay starting families and living on one's own becomes more popular. It is now around 380,000. The year 2002 was the first year since 1990 when more births than deaths were registered.

Dates in the history of Tallinn

1219 Danish forces under Waldemar II occupy Tallinn

1248 Tallinn joins Hanseatic League

Contexts

1346 Denmark sells Tallinn to the Teutonic Knights
1372 German replaces Latin as the official language
1422 Opening of Town Hall pharmacy, which still operates from the same site
1492 St Nicholas' Church receives its first legacy of silver
1524 First Lutheran sermon preached in Tallinn – at St Olav's
1535 The first catechism is published in Estonian
1561 Swedes occupy Tallinn
1591 5,000 people, about half the population, die from the Plague
1633 First British trading company, Thomas Clayhills, opens
1684 Much of Old Town destroyed in a fire
1710 Russian army under Peter the Great seizes Tallinn
1772 Tallinn's first newspaper is published, in German
1790 Swedish navy fails to seize Tallinn from the Russians
1820 Census gives population as 13,000 with 5,500 Germans, 4,400 Estonians and
      2,300 Russians
1854 British and French blockade harbour during Crimean War
1870 Railway to St Petersburg opened
1887 Russian replaces German as the language of instruction in all schools
1905 Frequent protests and strikes against Tsarist regime
1908 Tsar Nicholas II and King Edward VII meet on their yachts in Tallinn harbour
1910 A statue of Peter the Great is erected to celebrate 200 continuous years of
      Tsarist rule

History

1917   Bolsheviks seize Tallinn from Germans

1918   Estonian independence declared on February 24

1919   Royal Navy establishes base on Naissaar Island in Tallinn harbour

1920   Tartu Peace Treaty in February brings war with USSR to an end

1924   An attempted coup by 300 armed communists is crushed on December 1

1928   Performance of first Estonian opera

1931   First 'Miss Estonia' contest held

1937   First of two British-built submarines delivered in Tallinn harbour to the Estonian navy

1938   Tallinn census gives population as 146,000 and notes 17 hotels and 25 foreign legations in the town. Extensive celebrations mark the 20th anniversary of Estonian independence

1939   Baltic-German families all forced to 'return home' to Germany

1940   Soviet forces occupy Tallinn on June 16

1941   German forces occupy Tallinn on August 28

1944   Soviet forces reoccupy Tallinn on September 22

1950   Population of Tallinn reaches 200,000

1955   First television programmes transmitted in Estonian

1965   Twice-weekly ferry service opens to Helsinki and for 25 years will be its only link abroad

1980   Olympic Games sailing events held in Tallinn

1989   Estonian flag is raised on Tall Hermann Tower on February 24

1991 Estonian government formed in Tallinn
1994 Last Russian troops leave Tallinn
2002 Eurovision Song Contest held in Tallinn

POLITICS

Estonia nationally and Tallinn locally has been governed since independence in 1991 by a rapidly changing series of coalitions. Yet these are hardly noticed outside the country as few policy disputes impinge on foreign tourists or business visitors. Some mayors, emulating Jacques Chirac in Paris or Willy Brandt in Berlin, have used the position as an entrée into national politics. Others have followed Ken Livingstone in London to use it as an alternative power base. The articles that fill the local papers would have a familiar ring to residents in any large western European city, were they able to read them. Accusations of incompetence, of personal greed and of corruption are the regular fare. The few parts of Old Tallinn with roads wide enough for cars tried a congestion charge but then gave it up. It took at least a year to decide how much space under a major square a car-park and a bus station should have between them. Funds and programmes for drug rehabilitation on the 'sink' estates are always inadequate.

If tourists are coming to Tallinn from all over the world, the residents can hardly yet be called cosmopolitan. Roughly 60% are ethnically Estonian and the other 40% Russian. They hardly mix and few Russians are in senior jobs. With any Estonian over 30 still having bitter memories of Soviet times, it is not surprising that no signs

Politics

are in Russian, that the public sector works exclusively in Estonian and that some knowledge of Estonian is a requirement for citizenship. Russians unable or unwilling to learn Estonian are doomed to endure the jobs that in other countries are imposed on immigrants, in other words, ones locals can always avoid for something better paid and more comfortable.

ECONOMICS

There has been broad agreement amongst all political parties on the country's general economic framework and from 2004 this will in any case be largely determined by Brussels. Unlike other former Soviet republics, Estonia never had any doubts about plunging immediately into a capitalist economy and it established a tax system which encouraged extensive foreign investment. The public sector withdrew from agriculture and industry and to some extent also from transport. Visitors who travel to the suburbs will notice competitive bus companies operating on similar routes. The kroon instantly replaced the Russian rouble in 1992, whereas in the two neighbouring Baltic countries transitional currencies were maintained for another year. The kroon was tied to the German mark and has kept to the same peg with the euro. Value added tax was not only introduced but was collected too. Worries as the country is about to enter the EU centre on the role that Finland and Sweden will play in the economy as manufacturing, distribution and land ownership is less and less in Estonian hands.

PEOPLE

Nothing hurts Estonians more than to be called Russians or Balts. They have minimal interest in either Russia or Latvia and their language is close to that of the Finns. They are not interested in small talk, preferring to get to the point quickly. In business, they are not aggressive, feeling that a calmer approach is more likely to get results. In print, they are more serious than British writers tend to be, so do not expect any caustic asides or irony in the locally produced guidebooks or histories. (Those produced by the Estonian Institute are a welcome exception.) As most families lost several members to the Siberian prison camps in the 1941 and 1949 deportations, it is not surprising that many still feel resentful towards any Russian they meet.

The local community

Tallinn is rigidly divided between the 60% of the population who speak Estonian and the 40% who speak Russian. Seeing so little written in Russian, it is hard to believe that they form such a large percentage of the population. This virtual ban on its use is an understandable reaction to 50 years of Soviet occupation. The Russians are largely restricted to menial jobs that Estonians no longer wish to do. Expect to find them as chambermaids, shop assistants and waiters but not in offices or at the reception desks of grand hotels. Russians who want to get on in Tallinn learn Estonian as quickly as possible and try to put their past behind them.

People

TALLINN IN 1960
Michael Bourdeaux

For 15 years after World War II, Tallinn was a closed city, nestling amongst the forest of defensive (offensive) weaponry trained on the NATO countries. Suddenly in 1960 it was opened to Western visitors. I was lucky enough to have been a student at Moscow University at the time, so in May 1960 I was perhaps the first British visitor. I not only went there by train from Leningrad but also stayed illegally in a private house for the first and only time during the 25 years that I knew the Soviet Union. Far from being worried that I would bring trouble on their heads, the occupants barred the exit and refused to let me out until I had agreed to stay for three nights, having found my photograph displayed on their wall!

All of us, as if by common agreement, steered clear of the topic of the Soviet occupation but the family thoroughly organised my time for the next three days. After eight months in drab winter Moscow, the élan of ancient Tallinn in its bright spring colours took me into a new world. A visit on Sunday to Kaide's

Estonians do not react in any special way when dealing with foreigners. So many have relatives abroad, and/or have now left the country themselves for holidays or to work, that they speak English, see English-speaking films and have no problem in

Lutheran church, St Charles' Church, left mixed impressions. Strangely, the family did not want to accompany me. This huge church was about half full, with 40% of the congregation younger people, a far higher proportion than one saw in Russia. I tried to see the pastor after the service, but the corridor was blocked by dozens of young people waiting outside his door. None of these, to my surprise, would speak to me, although most must have known Russian. I surmised they were waiting for religious instruction, illegal under the Soviet system at the time, and were unwilling for a foreigner (or a Russian if they took me for one) to intrude.

On my final day, having purchased an air ticket to Riga, I was waiting on the tarmac beside a small aeroplane. An official came up to me, demanded my documents, took me inside and told me my intended flight was illegal for a foreigner. 'Our rules are less strict than yours in Britain for Soviet citizens,' he said. 'When I was there, I was prevented from visiting many places. You can go where you like, but not always by your chosen route. Visit Riga by all means, but you must do so by train via Leningrad.'

relating to outsiders. In fact, absorbing Western food and brand names and indulging in the consumer culture is a further mechanism for distancing themselves from the Soviet past and the Russian present.

People

RELIGION

As the church had a somewhat underground role in the Soviet period, it is difficult to give a clear picture of religious allegiance, both then and in contemporary Estonia. A few Lutheran and Orthodox churches continued to function after 1945 but many were converted to other uses and there was no religious education in schools. Most reopened again either during the perestroika era or after the restoration of independence, but funding remains a great problem. Of the 20% of the population who profess to religious convictions, about half are Lutheran and half Orthodox. The Orthodox community is divided into an Estonian and Russian one. Tallinn, unlike Riga or Vilnius, never had a large Jewish community and so was spared the worst brutality of the Holocaust.

Local charities

The culture of volunteering has yet to catch on in Estonia. Perhaps as one of the few Soviet legacies still remaining, the state continues to be seen as responsible for any initiative in the public sector. It is therefore very difficult to generate community interest in say improvements for a school or church. In the immediate aftermath of independence, the Estonian community abroad funded many projects in the public sector, as did the EU. Although many Estonians at home could now take this on, they do not do so. Perhaps those who see how active volunteers are elsewhere will start to generate similar behaviour in Estonia.

BUSINESS

Most foreigners are pleasantly surprised by the directness of the Estonian approach to business. They will want to establish quickly whether there is common ground and they do not waste time on small talk; in other words, the approach is the complete opposite of that used in many Asian countries. They are happy to talk shop over a light lunch but will not expect glamorous evenings to be part of the negotiating pattern. For business purposes, there is no need to waste time trying to learn a few words of Estonian. These will probably be misunderstood anyway as so few foreigners can speak the language with a remotely acceptable accent. English is the normal language of business with foreigners and even between Estonians, and ethnic Russians as Estonians are very reluctant to admit to knowing Russian.

CULTURE AND FESTIVALS

With the three Baltic states, it is normally easier to say what divides them rather than what unites them. However, a passion for choral singing, initially started as a protest movement against Tsarist rule, was continued during the first period of independence (1918–40) and shows no signs of abating now. The Song Festival which takes place every four years in Tallinn used to be a barometer of Soviet control. Political analysts observed every word, every gesture and the colours of the performers' clothes. Blue, black and white represented the banned national flag. Now it reflects a genuine commitment to music and the next Song Festival in summer 2004 is likely to host over 20,000 participants and 250,000 visitors.

Culture and festivals

For most of the year, visitors to Tallinn can be sure their visit will coincide with an annual music festival. Organ music, jazz and dancing are regular features and Estonian pop singers now compete with famous names from abroad for loyal audiences at the Saku Suurhall, venue of the 2002 Eurovision Song Contest. As Tallinn hotels are full during the peak summer months, more and more festivals are arranged at other times of year. Before booking a holiday, visitors should check the Tallinn Tourist Board website www.tourism.tallinn.ee to see what is on when they plan to go, and perhaps consider changing their dates.

GEOGRAPHY AND CLIMATE

Tallinn, with the Old Town based around a hillside, gives a misleading impression of Estonia as a whole. The rest of the town and the rest of the country are very flat indeed. The highest point in Estonia is just 300m above sea level. It is a hill near the Latvian border which is referred to locally as a mountain, since by comparison with the rest of the country, it represents such a protruding landmark. Tallinn is situated on a bay which contains several islands. Two of these, Aegna and Naissaar, had thriving fishing communities until World War II, then became secret Soviet bases and are now reinventing themselves as nature reserves.

Climate

Tallinn is fortunate that it is reached by the Gulf Stream. Whilst for much of the winter temperatures do fall below freezing, days when they fall below −10°C are few and far between. Global warming has of course also made the winters milder, so whilst ice-breakers are still needed to keep the harbour open, they are no longer in daily use. Spring and autumn are short seasons in Estonia, with winter weather common from mid-October until April. From March to May and September to October, expect temperatures of 10–20°C in the daytime. Summer can be said to start in mid-May and continue until mid-September. The weather is changeable throughout the summer, with bright sunshine often turning suddenly to rain within an hour or so. Temperatures are pleasantly mild in comparison with those around the Mediterranean at that time, unlikely to drop below 15°C. The norm is 20–25°C, with heatwaves – up to 30°C – being rare.

Current weather in Tallinn and forecasts for the next few days can be checked on www.weather.ee/tallinn.

THE CITY – A PRACTICAL OVERVIEW

Tallinn has an ideal layout for the short-break visitor. Many tourists will never need a bus or a taxi, with everything they need to see within walking distance of most hotels. Staying around Toompea, the hill on which old Tallinn is built, can occupy a leisurely three–four days' stay. Those with more time or who are staying in the suburbs will find public transport easy to use and taxis reasonably priced. Kadriorg Palace and the Rocca al Mare Open Air Museum are both on direct bus routes with a fare of 30p/50c. The long-distance bus station is halfway between the airport and the Old Town and is well served by local buses and trams. Day-to-day life is now totally Western so there is no need to shop in advance before coming; a forgotten toothbrush, a favourite tipple or an easy-read paperback can be bought seven days a week and even all around the clock. Indeed, most such items will be much cheaper than if bought at home.

Museums still open and close to suit the staff rather than visitors. Most close at least one day a week – usually Monday or Tuesday – and some take two days off. They also close on public holidays. If visiting one is crucial to your holiday, check first that it is open when you plan to be there. Churches are, of course, open every day so they can always provide the backbone to a visit.

In 2002 and 2003 Tallinn became so popular as a short-break destination and a conference centre that hotels became full all week, all year-round. Last-minute discounts were unheard of and the best prices were always paid by those who booked their packages well in advance. Airlines introducing new services to Tallinn quickly found them filling up at what they considered to be sensible fares, a pleasant contrast to so many other routes. However, 900 new hotel rooms are due to open in 2004 and the no-frills carriers are expressing an interest in the Baltics so this situation may well then change to the benefit of the tourist.

WHEN TO VISIT

Tallinn is a very different city in the two major seasons of winter and summer. In the former, tourists enjoy themselves largely indoors around a programme of concerts, ballet and filling meals. In the summer, when daylight reduces the night to an hour or two, the attractions are all out of doors. Some visitors probably spend their whole stay on Town Hall Square now that so much entertainment is centred there, but the more sensible will climb the walls and towers, meander through the Kadriorg Palace Gardens and take bus trips along the seashore.

Summer visitors are entertained with brass bands, fancy dress and outdoor singing. Winter ones are inspired with organ recitals, opera and chamber music. Serious Estonians take long summer holidays so do not expect much culture in Tallinn in July or August. It is the season to unwind and have fun.

SUGGESTED ITINERARIES
One day

Spend the whole day in the Old Town starting at the top of the Toompea Hill around 09.00 when the churches open but before the cruise passengers are brought there. Start at the Alexander Nevsky Cathedral (page 119 [3 B6]), continue to the Dome

Church (page 120 [3 B5]), walk down Lühike jalg ('Short Leg') and drop into the Adamson-Eric Museum (page 89 [3 C5]) at the bottom of the hill to be amazed at how one man can produce art in so many shapes and forms. A visit to Niguliste Church (St Nicholas') (page 122 [3 C5]) should finish the morning.

Tallinn Old Town

Spend midday around Town Hall Square and, if the weather permits, climb the Town Hall Tower for a view of contemporary Tallinn before going down to the basement (page 117 [2 C4]) to see the exhibition on how the square has looked over the last 800 years. Do not forget to use the toilets here as they offer the best views of the foundations.

Continue the afternoon at the City Museum (page 105 [2 C3]) and allow an hour to watch all the films which relive the bombing in 1944 and the independence demonstrations in 1988–91. Have a cup of tea in the café at the top and then finish up at the Maritime Museum (page 112 [2 C1]) to see how and why so many nations fought for control of the harbour. Only the British (and the Estonians!) are presented in a favourable light. The latest exhibit covers the tragedy of the *Estonia* which sank in September 1994, claiming 850 lives. The two streets that link the museum to the Viru Gate, Uus and Müürivahe, are ideal for a final stroll, as they have a range of buildings to admire, but also small cafés and shops. Do take a walk around the Old Town after sunset to see the major buildings bathed in floodlight.

Suggested itineraries

Two days

After a totally urban day, some greenery is called for, so start by taking the tram to Kadriorg Palace (page 137 [1 D2]) and linger in the gardens before going in. Do not miss the porcelain at the Mikkeli Museum (page 139 [1 D2]) before walking on as far as the Song Festival Grounds (page 136 [1 E1]). Try to imagine 5,000 people singing here, or come in July 2004 or July 2009 and see the real thing. Take the bus back to Vabaduse Väljak (Freedom Square, page 97 [3 D6]), an area where there are many cafés for lunch. Look in at the Tallinn Art Hall to see which contemporary artists are in favour, and then face the Occupation Museum (page 114 [3 C7]) which shows the horrors and banalities of life under the Soviet and German occupations between 1940 and 1991. Finish the afternoon at the National Library (page 112 [3 C8]). Hopefully there will be a concert in the early evening either at Niguliste (page 122 [3 C5]) or at the Dome Church (page 120 [3 B5]).

TOUR OPERATORS

In the UK, an increasing number of city-break operators are adding Tallinn to their programmes. They are joining operators who have specialised in the Baltic states since their independence. Those in the latter category offer both short breaks and longer tours around the country. Operators listed outside the UK, of course, offer more extensive programmes than city breaks, given the time passengers are likely to spend in the area. Passengers arriving late in the evening at the airport should ensure that their travel agent books an arrival transfer as there may not be enough taxis for all the passengers who want them. All operators listed below have several years' experience in the area and are fully bonded to protect the money clients have paid. They will not only have reduced airfares to the area, but often also lower hotel prices than those generally available to the public.

UK city-break operators
Bridge Travel Bridge House, 55–59 High Rd, Broxbourne, Herts EN10 7DT; tel: 0870 191 7270; fax: 01992 456609; email: info@bridgetravel.co.uk; web: www.bridgetravel.co.uk
Cresta Tabley Court, Victoria St, Altrincham WA14 1EZ; tel: 0870 238 7711; fax: 0161 385 4059; email: cresta@crestaholidays.co.uk; web: www.crestaholidays.co.uk
Kirker Holidays 3 New Concordia Wharf, Mill St, London SE1 2BB; tel: 020 7231 3333; fax: 020 7231 4771; email: cities@kirkerholidays.com; web: www.kirkerholidays.com
Traveleditions 69–85 Tabernacle St, London EC2A 4BD; tel: 020 7251 0045; fax: 020 7251 7399; email: tours@traveleditions.co.uk; web: www.traveleditions.co.uk
Travelscene 11–15 St Ann's Rd, Harrow, Middx HA1 1LQ; tel: 0870 777 9987; fax: 020 8861 4154; email: admin@travelscene.co.uk; web: www.travelscene.co.uk

Baltic specialists
UK
Baltic Holidays 40 Princess St, Manchester M1 6DE; tel: 0870 757 9233; fax: 0870 120 2973; email: info@balticholidays.com; web: www.balticholidays.com
Fregata Travel 83 Whitechapel High St, London E1 7QX; tel: 020 7247 8484; fax: 020

7247 7884; email: fregata@commodore.co.uk; web: www.fregatatravel.co.uk

Operas Abroad The Tower, Mill Lane, Rainhill, Prescot, Merseyside L35 6NE; tel/fax: 0151 493 0382; email: info@operasabroad.com; web: www.operasabroad.com

Regent Holidays 15 John St, Bristol BS1 2HR; tel: 0117 921 1711; fax: 0117 925 4866; email: regent@regent-holidays.co.uk; web: www.regent-holidays.co.uk

Specialised Tours 4 Copthorne Bank, Copthorne, Crawley, West Sussex RH10 3QX; tel: 01342 712785; fax: 01342 717042; email: info@specialisedtours.com; web: www.specialisedtours.com

Special Places 18–24 Westbourne Grove, London W2 5RH; tel: 0870 499 0311; fax: 020 7313 6601; email: sales@specialplaces.co.uk; web: www.specialplaces.co.uk

Vamos Fernwood House, Brindly Brae, Kinver, West Midlands DY7 6LR; tel: 01384 878125; fax: 0870 762 1016; email: info@vamostravel.com; web: www.vamostravel.com

US

Amest Travel 16 Ocean Parkway #19, New York 11218; tel: 718 972 2217; fax: 718 851 4175; email: info@amest.com; web: www.amest.com

Value World Tours Plaza del Lago Building, Suite 203, 17220 Newhope St, Fountain Valley, CA 92708; tel: 714 556 8258; fax: 714 556 6125; email: vmmail@vwtours.com; web: www.vwtours.com

Vytis Tours 40–24 235th St, Douglaston, New York 11363; tel: 800 778 9847 or 718 423 6161; fax: 718 423 3979; email: tours@vytistours.com; web: www.vytistours.com

Canada

Valhalla Travel and Tours 120 Newkirk Rd, Unit 25, Richmond Hill, Ontario C4C 9S7; tel: 800 265 0459 or 905 737 0300; fax: 905 737 0304; email: info@valhallatravel.com; web: www.valhallatravel.com

RED TAPE

By 1994, only three years after re-establishing independence, Estonia had become a Western country. Visas for most tourists had been abolished or were easily available on arrival, red and green exits at customs had been established and the major Scandinavian chains were marketing their goods all around the country. Visitors coming to Tallinn early in the 21st century will find it hard to visualise what a backwater it had become for much of the 20th, when the Soviet Union first banned completely and then severely restricted all contacts with foreigners.

Visitors from all EU countries, Australia, Canada, New Zealand, Norway, Switzerland and the USA do not need visas and this list increases year by year. At the time of writing in late 2003, Estonia was not planning to join the Schengen Agreement so tourists who have a Schengen visa will still need to apply separately for an Estonian one. Up-to-date information is available on the Ministry of Foreign Affairs website www.vm.ee. Travellers who do need visas must get them from an Estonian embassy abroad so should plan their travel arrangements accordingly. They must take account of both local and Estonian holidays when embassies may be closed.

Red tape

Estonian embassies

For embassies in Tallinn, see page 38.

Australia 86 Louisa Rd, Birchgrove, New South Wales 2041; tel: 2 9810 7468; fax: 2 9818 1779; email: eestikon@ozemail.com.au

Canada Suite 210, 260 Dalhousie St, Ottawa K1N 7E4; tel: 613 789 4222; fax: 613 789 9555; email: estonianembassy@rogers.com; web: www.estemb.ca

Finland Itainen Puistotie 10, Helsinki 00140; tel: 9 622 0260; fax: 9 622 0261; email: embassy.helsinki@mfa.ee; web: www.estemb.fi

France 46 Rue Pierre Charron, Paris 75008; tel: 1 56 62 22 00; fax 1 49 52 05 65; email: embassy.paris@mfa.ee; web: www.est-emb.fr

Germany Hildebrandstrasse 5, 10785 Berlin; tel: 30 254 60600; fax: 30 254 60601; email: embassy.berlin@mfa.ee; web: www.estemb.de

Ireland Riversdale House, Ailsbury Rd, Dublin 4; tel: 1 219 6730; fax: 1 219 6731; email: embassy.dublin@mfa.ee

Latvia Skolas 13, Riga 1010; tel: 781 2026; fax: 781 2029; email: embassy.riga@mfa.ee

Lithuania Mickeviciaus 4a, Vilnius 2004; tel: 2 78 02 00; fax: 2 78 02 01; email: embassy.vilnius@mfa.ee

South Africa 16 Hofmeyr St, Welgemoed 7530; tel: 21 913 3850; fax: 21 933 2579

UK 16 Hyde Park Gate, London SW7 5DG; tel: 020 7589 3428; fax: 020 7589 3430; email: embassy.london@mfa.ee; web: www.estonia.gov.uk

USA 2131 Massachusetts Av, Washington DC 20008; tel: 202 588 0101; fax: 202 588 0108; emb.washington@mfa.ee; web: www.estemb.org

GETTING THERE AND AWAY
By air

From around 2000, **Estonian Air** (UK tel: 020 7333 0196; web: www.estonian-air.ee) embarked on a programme of massive expansion, firstly in the hands of Maersk Air and then from 2003 under the ownership of SAS. By early 2004, it had direct flights to Amsterdam, Berlin, Copenhagen, London, Paris and Stockholm, usually on a daily basis. CSA Czech Airlines, Finnair, Lufthansa and SAS also have regular services. Travel agents specialising in the area can also arrange for flights to Tallinn, combined with a one-way fare from another town in the Baltics. Travellers from the British Isles who do not live in London can take advantage of Lufthansa and SAS flights from Birmingham, Dublin, Edinburgh, Glasgow and Manchester to Copenhagen, Frankfurt or Stockholm and then change to Tallinn services there. CSA also operate from Birmingham, Manchester and Edinburgh; with a careful choice of flights it is possible to have the best part of a day in Prague en route to Tallinn.

Fares fluctuate frequently and for short-break visitors it is often cheaper to book a package than flights and hotels separately. Low-cost carriers may start services to Estonia in 2004 from Britain, Germany and Sweden. The lowest fares are usually available in winter, spring and autumn, but invariably increase over Christmas and Easter. To secure reasonable prices in the summer, it is important to book well in advance. When in Tallinn, Estonian Air have a dedicated phone number for English speakers, tel: 640 1163, which is available 09.00–20.00 seven days a week. Their website is www.estonian-air.ee

For travellers from the USA, SAS and Finnair offer good connections, again via Copenhagen and Stockholm, but given the very low fares usually available to London from Canada and the USA, it may often be cheaper to break a journey in London and take a separate package from there. Via London is always the best route for tourists from Australia and New Zealand.

By helicopter from Helsinki

An hourly service to Helsinki operates Monday–Friday between 07.30 and 20.00 from the heliport on the roof of the Linnahall Concert Hall, next to the seaport. Flying time is 18 minutes. A reduced service operates at weekends. Various fares are offered and journeys starting in Tallinn are usually cheaper than those starting in Helsinki. For a round-trip journey, expect to pay £120–180/US$180–270. Discounts are also offered for reservations made in advance. This can be done through most travel agents or directly with the company operating the service, **Copterline**, whose office is at the heliport; tel: 610 1818; fax: 641 2276; email: copterline@copterline.ee; web: www.copterline.ee. Another booking office opened in 2004 in the Viru Hotel.

By ferry from Helsinki

Competition between an increasing number of companies on the Tallinn–Helsinki route ensures a year-round comprehensive service, supplemented in the summer by catamarans which reduce the journey time to 90 minutes. Most ferries take about three to four hours and in good weather the views of Helsinki and Tallinn make this journey really worthwhile. As fares change frequently, tickets are best bought from agents in either Helsinki or Tallinn who will know the full range available. Expect to pay around £20–30/US$30–45 for a round-trip ticket. The Tallinn port website www.portoftallinn.com is the best starting point for an indication of services and fares. **Eckerö**, **Silja Line** and **Tallink** are the main ferry companies whilst **Linda Line** and **Nordic Jet** run the catamarans.

Given the speed of the catamarans, a day-trip in summer to Helsinki is a very practical add-on to a visit to Tallinn. Money can be exchanged on board but exchange rates are poor so it is better to use banks or bureaux de change in either town centre. Tallinn port is within walking distance of the town and metered taxis are always available. Local buses are few and far between at the port itself but several routes operate within 400 metres or so of the port entrance.

By bus

The bus station (**Autobussijaam**) for domestic and international departures is on Lastekodu, off the Tartu Road which leads to the airport. The phone number for enquiries is 680 0900 but do not expect English to be spoken.

Eurolines are the main operator of international services although they are now beginning to face competition. They operate five times a day to both Riga and St Petersburg and keep to their timetables as they always have priority at the border. Some of the buses to Riga continue to Vilnius and Minsk. Their timetables are available on line at www.eurolines.ee and they are also published in *Tallinn In Your*

Getting there and away

Pocket. Tickets cannot be booked online so this should be done through travel agents before arrival or at their office at the bus station in Tallinn. Tickets booked at the bus station will cost about £10/US$15 to St Petersburg and £8/US$12 to Riga but agents will of course add a service charge to this.

There is an extensive domestic bus service from Tallinn to towns all over Estonia. Fares right across the country will not exceed £6/US$9 and full timetables and fares are displayed at the bus station. It is not normally necessary to book in advance but this should be done for services on Friday and Sunday evenings and also on major holidays. Only one-way tickets are sold so the return ticket to Tallinn should be bought on arrival at the destination. On the main routes there is competition and savings can be made by adjusting travel timings to the buses of the cheaper operators.

By train

Rail services within Estonia and to neighbouring countries have consistently declined since independence and are unlikely to be of any use to visitors. The only international services now operate overnight to St Petersburg and to Moscow and these need to be booked well in advance in conjunction with accommodation, as the Russian visa insists upon specific dates and places for entry and exit.

HEALTH

Standards of care in hospitals are very high and, to ensure no hiccoughs in joining the EU, health and safety inspections in restaurants and hotels are probably of a higher level than those carried out in countries already in the EU. Water is safe to drink everywhere, although from the quantity of bottles sold in kiosks, the impression one gets is that this is not the case. The British NHS has no reciprocal arrangements with Estonia and health insurance is in theory mandatory for all foreign visitors.

SAFETY

Violent crime is very rare in Tallinn although drunken brawls late on Friday and Saturday nights can be unpleasant. It is, however, easy to avoid the rowdy clubs which generate these. Pickpockets are a problem in markets during the summer when the hordes of cruise passengers provide plenty of temptation. The 'sink' estates where, perhaps inevitably, the drug culture thrives are fortunately well away from the areas visited by tourists. Women will not feel uncomfortable walking on their own.

MONEY
Currency

The Estonian kroon is tied to the euro at the rate of 15.65EEK. (It was fixed at 8.00EEK to the German mark when it replaced the Russian rouble in 1992 and has stayed at this rate ever since.) In April 2004 exchange rates against the pound and US dollar were £1 = 23.85EEK and US$1 = 13.00EEK. Notes are issued for 1, 2, 5, 10, 25, 50, 100 and 500EEK although those for one and two kroon are now being replaced with coins. There are also coins for 10, 20 and 50 sents.

Money

Budgeting

Hotel costs in Tallinn will be similar to those in western Europe or the US, outside the big cities. Do, however, remember that room rates always include a substantial buffet breakfast. All other expenditure, mainly meals and transport, will be much cheaper. Allow around 50p/80c for coffee and a similar amount for cakes. Estonians have not yet adopted take-away food on a large scale; they either prepare it in their offices and homes or eat out. Restaurants do not offer set-price meals so eating is always à la carte. Great savings can be made by avoiding wine with meals and drinking beer instead. Most restaurants charge the same at lunch as in the evening although a few glamorous restaurants have a 'business lunch' to encourage midday trade. In most restaurants in central Tallinn allow about £2/US$3 for a starter, £5/US$8 for the main dish and £3/US$5 for the sweet. Much lower prices can be found away from the Old Town and the port where prices are governed by the number of tourists and ex-pats in the area.

Many tourists use a taxi or public transport only to get to and from the airport. Most hotels are within walking distance of many of the sights tourists will want to visit. As a carnet of ten bus tickets costs 70EEK (£3/US$5), little needs to be allowed for travel for those who venture further.

Tipping

It is normal to leave 10% in restaurants, cafés, taxis and hairdressers when the service is good. Many ex-pats make a point of not tipping if the service does not deserve it, in the hope that it will improve on future occasions!

Planning

BANKS AND CREDIT CARDS

The **Äripank** at Vana Viru 7, close to the Viru Gate [2 E3], usually gives the best exchange rate for pounds and dollars. The nearby **Tavid** Exchange at Aia 5 [2 E3] is very useful for getting rid of unwanted notes from all over the world. During the day, their rates are as good as those at Äripank and they do not charge commission so even small amounts can sensibly be exchanged. Tavid is open around the clock but from 19.00 until 09.00 the following day during the week, and from 17.00 at the weekends, their rates worsen considerably, often by as much as 10%. Elsewhere in the town, both at banks and exchange bureaux, the rate for pounds can vary enormously whereas that for dollars is less erratic. There are many exchange bureaux and banks along Viru [2 D4] which leads from Viru Square to Town Hall Square. Check the rates before deciding which to use. The exchange bureaux are open daily from 10.00 until 19.00. Banks close at 17.00 or 18.00 and do not usually open at weekends. ATMs (cashpoints) are available throughout the town.

Appalling rates for all currencies can always be guaranteed at the 'airside' bureau in Tallinn airport and at the bus station so these two outlets should be avoided. The banks 'landside' at the airport and those at the railway station offer reasonable rates. Tourists are advised not to accept notes of 500EEK when changing money since they are often difficult to use as most transactions will involve much smaller sums or can be paid by credit card.

Tourists from Britain can obtain kroon at Gatwick Airport before they leave and from all major banks. They are also available in Helsinki. This also applies for the

Practicalities

two other Baltic currencies. Very few shops in Tallinn accept foreign currency, as it is technically illegal for them to do so.

Exchange bureaux never accept travellers' cheques and few banks do either. They are equally useless in shops and hotels. Leave them at home!

Credit cards

As credit cards are now widely used, there is no need to change large sums of money. Cards may be used in all hotels and restaurants, and in most shops. Few museums and galleries are able to accept them, although those that have opened recently usually do. Bus and train tickets, even those on international routes, have to be paid for in cash, but the cost of these is very low.

LOCAL MEDIA

The Baltic Times, published weekly on a Thursday, is the best English-language source of news for the three Baltic republics. It also lists exhibitions and concerts. *Tallinn In Your Pocket*, published every two months, is invaluable for its independent – and therefore irreverent – reviews on restaurants, museums and other sites. *The City Paper*, also published every two months, covers Tallinn, Riga and Vilnius together in a similar way to *Tallinn In Your Pocket* but with the addition of political articles. Both are a welcome contrast to many worthy but dull local guidebooks. Travel agents abroad who specialise in the Baltics will be able to provide copies of both publications or they are available online at www.inyourpocket.com and www.balticsworldwide.com.

Several free-of-charge listings magazines are circulated by hotels and local travel agents but as these are supported totally by advertising, they cannot be entirely trusted.

European editions of British and American newspapers are on sale in Tallinn at the larger hotels on the day of publication. The local daily business newspaper *Äripaev* has an English summary of its main stories.

There are no local radio or television stations that transmit in English.

COMMUNICATIONS
Telephones
Public phone boxes take only phone cards, which can be bought at kiosks. They do not take cash or credit cards. Calls can also be made from post offices. Mark-ups on phone calls from hotel rooms vary enormously. Some hotels have wisely reduced prices to persuade visitors not to use their mobile phones; others have kept charges that were acceptable in the 1990s but are not any longer. As in Britain, there is now no distinction in Estonia between costs for local or national calls, although some hotels still maintain one. From a phone box, reckon to spend about 50p/80c a minute to phone a landline in Britain or North America.

Dialling
To reach Tallinn by phone from abroad, dial the Estonia country code 372, the Tallinn city code of 6 and then the six-digit number. To reach phones abroad from Tallinn dial 00 and then the relevant country code.

Mobile phones

Many Estonians now have mobile phones, which are operated by a number of different companies. They each have a separate access code which is dialled after the 372 and which replaces the city code of 6. Despite the popularity of mobile phones, calls to and from them are still much more expensive than those to and from landlines.

The SMS craze has hit Tallinn more vigorously than most other cities. Such is the variety of services available that in autumn 2003 *Tallinn In Your Pocket* devoted a special section to this topic. Paying for car parks and checking bank balances this way is now old hat for Tallinners, as is checking the weather and finding a recipe for dinner. Recent additions include donating food for a baby elephant at Tallinn Zoo and buying condoms from machines that used to accept cash.

Useful telephone numbers

Ambulance and Fire Brigade	112
Central Hospital	620 7015
City Tourist Office	645 7777
Police	110
Telephone Information	626 1111

Post

The **Central Post Office** is at Narva mnt 1 [2 E3], opposite the Viru Hotel. It has relatively short opening hours, Monday–Friday 08.00–20.00 and on Saturday

08.00–18.00. It is closed on Sunday. It sells postcards, changes money and provides telephone services. Tourists often use the post office at the top of the Old Town at Lossi plats 4 [3 B3] beside the Alexander Nevsky Cathedral but this is only open 09.00–17.00 Monday–Friday. The postal service is extremely efficient, with cards reaching anywhere in Europe within a few days.

Internet

All major hotels have a business centre offering a full range of services including internet access but the charges are high – usually around 100EEK (£4/US$6) per half hour. Terminals are free of charge, but therefore often in use, at the National Library [1 B3]. Kaubamaja, the department store at the back of the Viru Hotel [2 D4], charges 40EEK (£1.75/US$3) an hour; the store is open seven days a week, Monday–Friday 09.00–21.00, Saturday 09.00–20.00 and Sunday 10.00–18.00. By far the cheapest centre in Tallinn is **Matrix** at Tartu 31, on the road to the bus station and airport. It charges only 15EEK (70p/US$1) an hour and is open day and night. The clientele is largely teenagers playing computer games and looking at sites which their parents would probably try to ban at home.

The computers which used to be available for free public use at the airport have been withdrawn. Only those passengers with access to the business lounges now have this facility.

EMBASSIES

Not all embassies have websites or public email addresses.

Canada Toom-Kooli 13; tel: 627 3311; fax: 627 3312; email: tallinn@canada.ee
Ireland Vene 2; tel: 681 1888; fax: 681 1899; email: embassytallinn@eircom.net
Latvia Tõnismägi 10; tel: 646 1313; fax: 631 1366
Lithuania Uus 15; tel: 631 4030; fax: 641 2013; email: amber@anet.ee; web: www.hot.ee/lietambasada
Russia Pikk 19; tel: 646 4175; fax: 646 4178; email: vensaat@online.ee; web: www.estonia.mid.ru
UK Wismari 6; tel: 667 4700; fax: 667 4723; email: information@britishembassy.ee; web: www.britishembassy.ee
USA Kentmanni 20; tel: 668 8100; fax: 668 8134; email: tallinn@usemb.ee; web: www.usemb.ee

HOSPITALS AND PHARMACIES

The Central Hospital (tel: 620 7015) on Ravi provides 24-hour emergency care and the 24-hour pharmacy (tel: 644 2282) is at Tõnismägi 5 [3 D8]. Long-gone are the days when foreigners who fell ill demanded to be taken immediately to Helsinki.

RELIGIOUS SERVICES

Tallinn now has an active religious life, with services held regularly at all the re-functioning churches in the Old Town. An English-language service is held every

Sunday at 15.00 at the Holy Ghost Church [2 C4]. Full details are available on www.eelk.ee/tallinna.puhavaimu. The synagogue is on Karu near the harbour. There is currently no mosque in Tallinn.

TOURIST INFORMATION

The **Tallinn Tourist Board** has a shop-front office on the corner of Kullassepa and Niguliste (St Nicholas') [3 C5] which sells a good range of books, maps and cards. They have up-to-date editions of *Tallinn In Your Pocket* and *The City Paper*. There is also a large reference folder with timetables for ferries to Finland, buses out of Tallinn and local railways. There is a similar office in the ticket hall by the harbour [1 B2]. This office, like all other tourist offices around Estonia, has a website: www.visitestonia.com. Visiting these sites before departure will save a lot of time on arrival.

For tourists who arrive without having pre-booked any excursions, or who need to book further accommodation in the Baltic area, the tourist office on the corner of Kullassepa 4/Niguliste 2 [3 C5] can advise on local operators with regular programmes. Recommended ones include:

Baltic Tours Pikk 31; tel: 630 0460; fax: 630 0411; email: incoming@baltictours.ee; web: www.bt.ee [2 C3]

Estonian Holidays Lai 5; tel: 627 0500; fax: 627 0501; email: holidays@holidays.ee; web: www.holidays.ee [2 B4]

Estravel Suur-Karja 15; tel: 626 6266; fax: 626 6262; email: sales@estravel.ee; web: www.estravel.ee [3 D5]

Tourist information

PUBLIC HOLIDAYS

New Year's Day	January 1
Independence Day	February 24
Midsummer	June 23–24
Restoration of Independence Day	August 20
Christmas Day	December 25

THE TALLINN CARD

Vigorously promoted by the tourist board and in many hotels, the Tallinn Card will suit visitors keen to visit many museums and to travel to the outlying attractions. The cost includes a free sightseeing tour, free use of public transport and free admission to all museums. For those still active in the evenings it also includes free admission to the Hollywood Nightclub. However, it has to be said that for those taking a more leisurely approach to their stay and who are based in the town centre, it may well be cheaper to pay as you go. No reductions in the cost are made on Mondays or Tuesdays when many museums are closed. Full details of what is included can be seen on web: www.tallinn.ee/tallinncard. From April 2004 the cost is 90EEK for 6 hours, 250EEK for 24 hours, 300EEK for 48 hours and 350EEK for 72 hours.

Practicalities

TALLINN AIRPORT

The airport is only 3–4km from the town centre. The current building dates originally from 1980 as Tallinn suddenly needed to show an international face for the Olympics (sailing events were held in the Baltic) and has been modernised on several occasions to meet the demands of Western travellers since independence. A local bus service operates to the town centre every quarter of an hour with the final stop behind the Viru Hotel. Several other hotels such as the Radisson and the Central are within walking distance of this stop. Tickets bought from the driver cost 15EEK (70p/US$1.10) and only local currency can be used. (Tickets bought from kiosks cost 10EEK individually or 70EEK if bought in a block of ten, but sadly the airport kiosk does not sell them.) During the day taxis are easily available. They are all metered and cost about 100EEK (£4.50/US$7) into town. Passengers arriving on late-evening flights should pre-book a transfer through their travel agent as few taxis operate then and the bus service usually finishes around 22.30. The local bus from the airport passes the main bus station (Autobussijaam), which is useful for those wanting to continue journeys beyond Tallinn. Local buses, transfer coaches and taxis must be paid for in local currency.

There is an exchange bureau airside and also one landside in the arrivals area. The landside one offers much better rates for incoming travellers. For travellers arriving from Britain on an Estonian Air flight from Gatwick, the Thomas Cook exchange bureau at Gatwick handles Estonian kroon. There is a cashpoint in the arrivals area. There is no tourist information office or hotel-booking agency at the airport. American and British tourists plagued by high airport taxes at home will be relieved to hear that at Tallinn airport they are minimal. Flight schedules are available on the website: www.tallinn-airport.ee.

TAXIS

Taxis are all metered and have a minimum fare of 35EEK. Journeys within town should not cost more than 50EEK. As taxis are reasonably priced and always metered, they can be considered for long journeys. For instance, one to Lahemaa National Park, about 100km from Tallinn, is unlikely to cost more than 800EEK (£36/US$60).

Taxi companies called by phone are always cheaper than those that ply for hire on the street or park at ranks. Their cars are a little older but perfectly safe and all have meters. Taxi Raadio (tel: 601 5111) is reliable and a journey to the airport with them rarely costs more than 50EEK.

LOCAL BUSES/TRAMS AND TROLLEYBUSES

Many tourists to Tallinn never take either a bus or a taxi during their stay as the Old Town is very close to most of the hotels and the steep narrow roads conveniently restrict traffic to pedestrians only anyway. Such visitors, however, miss everything that is cheaply and easily accessible by bus outside the Old Town. There are competing bus companies so exact routes and numbers change from time to time but services are frequent and the public transport map *Tallinn Ühistranspordi kaart*, published by Regio, is reprinted sufficiently often to be up to date. Some stops have maps but not all do and the names of the stops listed in the timetables are unlikely to mean much to visitors. The tram and trolleybus routes are of course fixed. In spring 2004 the flat fare was 10EEK for individual tickets bought from kiosks or 15EEK for tickets bought on the bus. A book of ten tickets bought at kiosks cost 70EEK, so buying one of these halves the cost of travel. Passes are available for stays of four days or longer. (See also *Tallinn Card*, page 40.) Good bus services operate to Pirita and Rocca al Mare and also to the cheaper suburban hotels such as the Dzingel and Susi. Tram enthusiasts will be pleased at the number of places relevant to tourists which their routes pass. For details of tram routes, see *map 4*.

CAR HIRE

This is not advisable within Tallinn. Distances are so short and parking so difficult that public transport and taxis are the sensible way to get around. Visitors planning to travel to other towns can easily rely on buses but cars are very useful for seeing the coast and national parks. In the summer it is important to pre-book cars as demand invariably exceeds supply. Tour operators abroad can easily do this, as can the local agents listed above, or bookings can be made directly with the many international and local companies now involved in this business.

Car hire

5

Tallinn now has about 60 hotels but they are often fully booked at weekends, during trade fairs and in the peak summer season. Pre-booking is therefore always advisable. Specialist travel agents abroad often have access to lower prices than those quoted by the hotels directly, and they may also have allocations at several hotels specifically reserved for them. February 2001 saw the opening of the Radisson and during 2002 and 2003 several smaller hotels opened in the Old Town and just outside it. The year 2004 will see the opening of the 200-room Tallink Hotel opposite the Viru Hotel, L'Ermitage next to the National Library and the Ülemiste beside the airport. Visitors wanting to 'outfinn the Finns' will be able to stay at the port at the Saku Hotel, named after Estonia's most famous brew. A glass will be offered at check-in and crates will be available for sale to take onto the nearby boats. It cannot be long before many major chains not yet represented in Tallinn (such as Hilton and Holiday Inn) establish themselves here.

The recommendations that follow are obviously rather arbitrary and omission of a hotel should in general be taken as resulting from lack of space rather than necessarily as a criticism. An ethical tour operator will be able to warn visitors away from the fortunately few hotels that have degenerated into brothels, which sadly cannot be listed as such here. It can be assumed in all cases that the rooms in the hotels mentioned below have private facilities, that the hotel accepts credit cards, and that it has a restaurant and bar. Many hotels have saunas which guests can use free of charge. Baths are rare in Estonian hotels, even in four-star establishments, so should be specifically requested.

PRICES

In luxury hotels expect to pay around £125/US$190 a night, in first class £70/UUS$120 and in tourist class £35–60/US$60–100. The more expensive hotels sometimes reduce prices at weekends and in July, the local holiday season, whereas the cheaper hotels usually increase them then. Prices always include buffet breakfast.

The prices quoted in EEK in this section should be taken as a rough indication of the price for a standard twin/double room with breakfast. Like airline fares, these vary enormously according to which agency makes the booking, the time of year, the day of the week and how far in advance the booking is made. The Estonian kroon is tied to the euro at a rate of ∈1 = 15.65EEK. In April 2004, £1 = 23.85EEK, US$1 = 13.00EEK.

Rock-bottom accommodation is hard to find in Tallinn, as is bed and breakfast. There is neither the wherewithal nor the will to make Tallinn backpacker friendly. Most Estonian families do not have a dining-room, let alone a spare bedroom, so cannot rent out rooms. Rundown buildings which elsewhere might be converted to hostels are in Tallinn quickly transformed into offices or exclusive private houses. The increasing number of small hotels that are opening is again unlikely to

Street scene

stimulate demand for inferior accommodation at a not much lower price. The *Tallinn In Your Pocket* website (www.inyourpocket.com) always has an up-to-date list of hostels and agencies for arranging long-stays in private houses.

LUXURY

Parkconsul Schlössle Pühavaimu 13/15; tel: 699 7700; fax: 699 7777; email: schossle@consul-hotels.com; web: www.consul-hotels.com [2 C3]
For several years, this hotel was in a class on its own but competition finally came in 2003 with the opening of the Three Sisters (see below). A townhouse owned by many successful Baltic Germans over the years, the Parkconsul Schlössle was converted into Tallinn's first truly luxurious hotel and any senior government minister from abroad has always stayed here. With just 27 rooms, it still maintains the air of a gracious private residence. There is a small conference centre, but it seems incongruous. The hotel is a setting for constant but unostentatious indulgence, for cigars rather than cigarettes, for champagne rather than wine. The restaurant, like all the best ones in Tallinn, is in a cellar and has an extensive menu. For those able briefly to abandon all this indulgence, the hotel is within walking distance of all the attractions in the Old Town. Double 3,350EEK.

Three Sisters Pikk 71; tel: 630 6300; fax: 630 6301; email: info@threesistershotel.com; web: www.threesistershotel.com [2 C2]
Perhaps because it is so luxurious, the hotel does not bother with an Estonian name as no Estonian could afford it. It is clearly aiming to rival the Parkconsul and is to some extent

modelled on it. Both buildings have a history of over five hundred years and both can claim famous rather than notorious owners. Here a library is the dominating public room and a member of staff escorts guests into the lift for the one-floor journey down to the restaurant. Having 23 rooms, one even with a piano, the atmosphere of a 19th-century townhouse can still be maintained. Computers and plenty of other 21st-century paraphernalia are available if needed, but it seems a pity to let modernity intrude. Estonians who wish to impress their friends on the cheap come for lunch here and linger over a £5/US$8 club sandwich. Foreigners come in the evening for pumpkin soup, pork with chanterelle mushrooms and a particular rarity in Estonia, homemade ice-cream. Double 5,550EEK.

FIRST CLASS

Barons Suur-Karja 7; tel: 699 9700; fax: 699 9710; email: barons@baronshotel.ee; web: www.baronshotel.ee [3 D5]

For every bank that closes in Tallinn, a new hotel opens, but in this case it is on the same site. Thirteen different banks in fact occupied the building during the 20th century. Some doors as a result do seem excessively secure. Visitors will find it hard to believe that Barons opened in 2003 rather than 1903, since the panelling, the minute lift, the sombre colour schemes and the illustrations of Tallinn are all from the earlier date. So is the name of the road: '*karja*' means 'to herd', as cattle used to be led to pasture along it. Whenever renovation is carried out, more and more papers from the early 20th century come to light. The view from many rooms and from the restaurant over the Old Town will again keep the 21st century away. For once it is sensible to go upstairs to eat in Tallinn, rather than downstairs. Do however avoid Friday and Saturday nights here, when the hotel is an oasis of quiet against a backdrop of raucous behaviour in the surrounding bars. No rooms have baths but the suites have jacuzzis. Double 2,500EEK.

Domina City Vana-Posti 11–13; tel: 681 3900; fax: 681 3901; email: city@domina.ee; web: www.dominahotels.com [3 D5]
As one of the few hotels to open in 2002, the Domina, with its Old Town location, its size and its standards, was bound to succeed. It is a pity that only six rooms have baths as well as showers, but the computers built into the television sets will be more than adequate compensation for most visitors, and the British will like the choice of Sky as well as BBC television. The Italian management is reflected in the ample use of marble in the reception area and with the range of wildly abstract art in the restaurant. What is distinctly not Italian is the fact that two whole floors are non-smoking. Like all good restaurants in Tallinn, the one here is built into a brick-lined cellar. Lovers of Soviet memorabilia should note the red star on the roof. Double 2,400EEK.

Meriton Grand Toompuiestee 27; tel: 667 7000; fax: 667 7001; email: hotel@grandhotel.ee; web: www.grandhotel.ee [3 A7]
Travellers who came to Tallinn in the early 1990s will remember the grim Hotel Tallinn that used to besmirch this site. Luckily all traces of it were removed before this new hotel opened in 1999. Being immediately below the Old Town and having 165 rooms, it appeals both to business travellers and to tourist groups. It is tempting to spend much of a stay in

First class

this hotel in the lift, since it offers one of the best views of Toompea Hill at the top of the Old Town. British tourists are drawn by the high proportion of rooms with baths. Double 3,000EEK.

Olümpia Liivalaia 33; tel: 631 5333; fax: 631 5325; email: olympia@revalhotels.com; web: www.revalhotels.com [1 A3]
Built originally for the Olympic Games in 1980, this hotel is now the firm favourite of foreign business visitors to Tallinn. With the range of restaurants and conference facilities it offers, some never leave the hotel during their stay in Tallinn. They are often joined by the local ex-pat community which has a particular affinity for the 60s' music played in the Bonnie and Clyde nightclub. At weekends and during the summer, rates drop to attract tourists paying their own way. All 400 rooms are now at least of four-star standard and the reception staff work very quickly during the arrival and departure 'rush hours'. The restaurant on the top floor offers excellent views of the Old Town and many rooms do so as well. The newspaper shop always stocks up-to-date British newspapers, a rarity in Tallinn. Tourists who want to arrive or leave in greater style than a local taxi is able to provide can hire the hotel's 9m-long Lincoln which costs about £50/US$80 an hour. Double 2,300EEK.

Reval Park Kreutzwaldi 23; tel: 630 5305; fax: 630 5315; email: sales@revalhotels.com; web: www.revalhotels.com [1 B3]
Formerly the dreaded Kungla Hotel which could barely claim two-star status, the site transformed itself within a few weeks during the summer of 1997 and has never looked

back. It has pioneered rooms for non-smokers, for the disabled and for those with allergies as well as round-the-clock gambling, fortunately in a casino with a separate entrance. Rooms are larger here than in most other hotels and the restaurant has very low prices for excellent food. Walking to the Old Town is just about possible and indeed essential as the surroundings are very bleak. The guarded car-park is free of charge to hotel guests. Double 2,000EEK.

St Petersbourg Rataskaevu 7; tel: 628 6500; fax: 628 6565; email: stpetersbourg@consul-hotels.com; web: www.consul-hotels.com [2 B4]
The St Petersbourg is under the same management as the de-luxe Schlössle Hotel and suits those who want a comfortable Old Town address and who do not miss luxury. Its location near to many famous clubs and restaurants appeals to visitors who can dispense with sleep for much of the night. It is one of the very few hotels in Tallinn to offer a baby-sitting service. Double 2,500EEK.

Santa Barbara Roosikrantsi 2a; tel: 640 7600; fax: 631 3992; email: st_barbara.res@scandic-hotels.ee; web: www.scandic-hotels.com [3 D7]
The austere limestone façade from the turn of the century hides a very professional operation which is run by the Scandic group who also operate the nearby Palace Hotel. The cellar restaurant is completely German, with no intrusion from Estonia or anywhere else. It has 53 rooms so staff get to know all the guests, many of whom are now regulars, which makes the hotel difficult to book for first-time visitors. Double 1,600EEK.

First class

Scandic Palace Vabaduse Väljak; tel: 640 7300; fax: 640 7299; email: palace@scandic-hotels.com; web: www.scandic-hotels.com [3 E7]

The hotel brochure claims it has offered 'excellent service since 1937' and this is probably true. Although many other hotels now match its facilities, Estonians are very loyal to it as the hotel was one of the few links from the first independence period that remained throughout the Soviet era. Embassies were briefly set up in the hotel in 1991 before foreign legations could reclaim their pre-war buildings. It is now equally conveniently situated for tourists interested in the Old Town and business visitors needing the government ministries. In 1997 President Meri opened the new Presidential Suite which will doubtless remain one of the most expensive in Tallinn at £250/US$400 per night, but the remaining 86 rooms are more modestly priced. The hotel is run by the Scandic Hotel Group that also operates the Santa Barbara in Tallinn, the Ranna in Pärnu and the Karupesa in Otepää. Double 2,600EEK.

Tallink Laikmaa 5; tel: 630 0800; fax: 630 0810; email: hotel@tallink.ee; web: www.tallink.ee [1 A3]

This large hotel will open in May 2004 on Viru Square at the edge of the rapidly developing commercial district.

Viru Viru Väljak 4; tel: 630 1390; fax: 630 1303; email: reservation@viru.ee; web: www.viru.ee [1 A3]

Being the centre of the tourism trade for much of the Soviet era, the enormous Viru initially found it hard to redefine its role in the face of competition and ever-rising standards. By

2000 it had finally undergone a complete renovation and can now serve both business clients and fastidious tourists. It has become very biased towards Finnish clients, some of whom can provide unwanted liveliness late on Friday and Saturday evenings. Its location is excellent for the Old Town and for local shops. Tourists determined to have a bath rather than a shower are more likely to succeed here. Although the hotel already had over 400 rooms, it opened an extension with a further 100 rooms in spring 2004. Double 2,500EEK.

TOURIST CLASS

Central Narva mnt 7; tel: 633 9800; fax: 633 9900; email: central@revalhotels.com; web: www.revalhotels.com [1 A2]

This hotel became an immediate favourite of tour operators from abroad when it opened in 1995 as it had no Soviet past to eliminate. Staff were immediately aware of the demands and eccentricities of Western tourists, who have been catered for in the café/restaurant ever since. The hotel offers disabled access and one room in the new wing is adapted for use by disabled guests. It is within easy walking distance of the Old Town and the main post office. Having opened in what was then a rundown part of town, the surrounding area is becoming increasingly attractive, with more shops and restaurants opening every year. Double 1,500EEK.

Dzingel Männiku 89; tel: 610 5201; fax: 610 5245; email: hotell@dzingel.ee; web: www.dzingel.ee

Situated in Nõmme, Tallinn's most exclusive suburb, the Dzingel is in fact one of the town's simplest and largest hotels. Regular long-stay visitors find its facilities perfectly

Tourist class

adequate in view of the low prices charged and many tourists are happy both in winter and in summer with its quiet location beside a pine forest. Modernisation in 2002 made a great difference. The bus journey north into the town centre takes about 20 minutes. It is one of the few hotels where the staff happily and openly speak Russian although they can manage basic English. The restaurant is dull and surprisingly expensive but there is a late-night supermarket in the same block which can provide the ingredients for a varied picnic. Double 700EEK.

L'Ermitage Toompuiestee 19; tel: 699 6400; fax: 699 6401; email: info@nordichotels.ee; web: www.nordichotels.ee [3 A7]

This hotel will open in summer 2004 and will be one of the closest to the Old Town to offer free parking facilities for its guests. With 91 rooms, it plans to attract tourist groups and visitors to the several nearby embassies.

Imperial Nunne 14; tel: 627 4800; fax: 627 4801; email: info@imperial.ee; web: www.imperial.ee [2 B4]

Like the Konventa Seta in Riga and the Rūdninkų in Vilnius, this hotel is built into the town wall, which is therefore being preserved as part of it. Although on one of the few real roads in the Old Town, the location is quiet, except in the restaurant/bar where the same tape of Irish music is played loudly 24 hours a day. Rooms vary greatly in size and protruding beams sometimes add more of the medieval ambience than some guests would wish. Double 2,200EEK.

Meriton Old Town Lai 49; tel: 614 1300; fax: 614 1311; email: hotel@grandhotel.ee [2 B1]
This 40-room hotel opened in March 2004 and is under the same management as the
Meriton Grand, but has deliberately been pitched at a very different clientele. Those who
normally shun two- or three-star hotels may well accept such a standard here, given the
view that most rooms have either over the Old Town, of St Olav's Church, or towards the
harbour. There is also the added appeal of the hotel being built into the city wall. Being on
the edge of the Old Town, the place is quiet yet with a reasonably central location, within
walking distance of many museums and shops. It is worth paying the slightly higher costs for
the rooms on the fourth floor, with their larger size, their baths rather than showers and
above all for the views. The basement rooms make up for the total lack of a view with the
skilfully implanted use of the old city wall. Double 1,000EEK.

Mihkli Endla 23; tel: 666 4800; fax: 666 4888; email: mihkli@anet.ee; web:
www.mihkli.ee [3 C8]
The location on one of the main roads leading from the town centre is certainly drab and
the hotel itself used to be as well. From around 1998, however, serious attempts were
made to improve the décor and the staff and these have been largely successful. It is within
walking distance of the Old Town and on the doorstep of the National Library. Long-stay
visitors are now here and locals use the restaurant, both of which are always a good sign.
The repeat business that the hotel enjoys is also evidence of a complete turn-around. The
live music at the weekends in the restaurant is of a consistently high standard and is well
soundproofed from the rest of the hotel. Double 900EEK.

Tourist class

Old Town Maestro Suur-Karja 10; tel: 626 2000; fax: 631 3333; email: maestro@maestrohotel.ee; web: www.maestrohotel.ee [3 D5]

Having opened in 2001, this small hotel now has its regulars who want straightforward furnishings, peace and quiet and yet an Old Town location. Rooms are much bigger than might be expected from a converted townhouse but the lift is much smaller – it can take only one person with a case at a time. The road is traffic-free but that does mean wheeling cases along the cobbles on arrival and departure. The reception area doubles up as a bar, which adds to the family atmosphere. The sauna and the business centre are, surprisingly, side by side on the top floor. Photographers should bring their cameras for the unusual views over the town from the staircase and from the sauna. Double 1,800EEK.

Pirita Convent Guesthouse Merivälja 18; tel: 605 5000; fax: 605 5010; email: pirita@osss.ee; web: www.piritaklooster.ee

For anyone determined to have quiet at night, this is undoubtedly the place to go for. The nuns stay up for late-comers so ideal guests are those who have dinner here and then go to their rooms. The yachting harbour of Pirita is 3km northeast of the town and the ruined convent with this new guesthouse is set well back from the main road. Prices, too, are provincial rather than Tallinn. Tourists with a car will be happy with the space here and others will be pleased that after 500 years a religious order is finally active on the site again. Double 1,000EEK.

Sakurock Sadama 25c; tel: 680 6600; fax: 680 6601; email: sales@sakurockhotel.ee; web: www.sakurockhotel.ee [1 B2]

This hotel will open in June 2004. As it is named after Tallinn's most famous brewery, it is hardly surprising that guests will be welcomed with a free glass and offered tours to the brewery. Being situated at the passenger ferry terminal, the hotel will be the closest one to Finland but the planned cuisine is Italian. The hotel will be two–three star but is under the same ownership as the deluxe Three Sisters in the Old Town. Perhaps it is just as well they are a mile apart; their respective clients would mix as well as beer on wine.

Skane Kopli 2c; tel: 667 8300; fax: 667 8301; email: skane@nordichotels.ee; web: www.nordichotels.ee [2 A3]

Being just over the railway and the tramlines from the Old Town, this hotel is literally on the wrong side of the tracks. Yet gentrification cannot be far away and in the meantime guests can enjoy prices that are half of those charged by hotels just 500m away. No rooms have baths, but all have BBC television. Try to get a room on the third floor rather than on the second since when the hotel opened in summer 2003 only the former had soundproofing. Double 800EEK.

Susi Peterburi 48; tel: 630 3300; fax: 630 3400; email: susi@susi.ee; web: www.susi.ee [1 E4]

An estate agent would probably describe the location as 'unprepossessing' since it is surrounded by factories and a petrol station and is on the wide St Petersburg motorway. It is literally the high point of Tallinn at 55m above sea level. On May 14 1343, the St George's Night rebellion took place here. It had started further north on April 23 and this was the nearest point to Tallinn that Estonian forces would reach. Over 10,000 were killed in a

Tourist class

desperate attempt to overthrow the Teutonic Knights. A plaque in the hotel lobby commemorates the battle, as does the park on the other side of the road where there are several further monuments. The hotel is more comfortable and more modern than any of the other tourist-class hotels outside the centre and is easily accessible by tram. The pictures displayed on its staircase put many of Tallinn's museums to shame. There are oils, lithographs and watercolours showing contemporary and historical Tallinn; other pictures are of country scenes. They are well lit and sensibly framed and of course can be seen 24 hours a day. Should the lift break down, this gallery is more than adequate compensation. The hotel suits many groups as parking is easy, as are access to the airport and the Tartu Road. Double 1,000EEK.

Taanilinna Uus 6; tel: 640 6700; fax: 646 4306; email: info@taanilinna.ee; web: www.taanilinna.ee [2 D3]
Perhaps they were daring, perhaps they were foolish, but in June 2002 Tallinn saw its first hotel with Russian-speaking reception staff and with brochures in English and Russian. The spelling 'Hotell' was the only concession made to Estonia at the time, although the website now has an Estonian section. Visitors who do not care about this will like the prices, the location in one of the few quiet streets in the Old Town and the use of wood rather than of stone. The terrace sadly looks out on to the back of a supermarket and a dreary block of flats but in future years this view may well change. The wine cellar is an unexpected bonus in a hotel of this size and category and is most welcome given the lack of other watering holes in the immediate vicinity. Double 1,500EEK.

Ülemiste Lennijamaa tee 2; tel: 603 2600; fax: 603 2601; email: sales@ylemistehotel.ee;
web: www.ylemistehotel.ee [1 D4]
This hotel is opening beside the airport in July 2004. With the number of flights arriving
late and leaving early, it will be a convenient location for many visitors. The regular airport
bus will stop outside the hotel and takes only 10 minutes to the town centre. As it will
have 132 rooms, the hotel will be able to cater for large groups and for those needing
parking space. Space too will predominate in the size of the lobby, the rooms and the
entrance. This should compensate for the lack of attractions within walking distance.
Double EEK1,000

Unique Paldiski mnt 3; tel: 660 0700; fax: 661 6176; email: info@uniquestay.com; web:
www.uniquestay.com [3 A7]
Tallinn hotels have tended to copy each other once a successful formula has been found.
The larger ones inevitably copy models from abroad and the smaller ones try to recreate a
1930s' ambience even though modern technology is around if guests need it. When the
Unique opened in spring 2003, it clearly wanted to break away from anything that had ever
been tried before. Each room has its own flat-screen computer which can be used free of
charge around the clock. It also has tea and coffee. The lighting in the corridors comes from
the floor rather than the ceiling. Orange rather than green or brown is the predominant
colour. Originally restricted to 17 rooms, the hotel added another 50 in April 2004. Several
of these, the Zen rooms, are as original as their predecessors, with whirlpool baths
adjustable lighting, and gravity-free chairs. This will also be the first hotel in Tallinn with an

Tourist class

Estonian restaurant! The chain plans to expand both within Tallinn and to the neighbouring Baltic states. Double EEK1,400.

Vana Wiru Viru 11; tel: 669 1500; fax: 669 1501; email: hotel@vanawiru.ee; web: www.vanawiru.ee [2 E4]

Viru St is always full of tourists but most will not know of the existence of this hotel as its entrance is at the back. It was one of the very few hotels to open in Tallinn during 2002. Its vast marble lobby suggests luxury but in fact the 80 rooms are of a standard size and mostly with showers rather than baths. Few have good views but with a location beside the city wall, one can forgive anything. Groups will like the convenient coach park right beside the entrance. Double 1,700EEK.

6

There is now such a choice of restaurants in Tallinn that it is invidious to attempt a shortlist. Every major nation is represented and more unusual ones include Argentina, Georgia, Lithuania and Scotland. Hawaiian and Thai food appeared for the first time in 2000, Czech and Arabic food followed in 2002 and by 2003 Russian food had also staged a comeback, having been completely rejected in the years immediately following independence. All restaurants and bars have to provide a non-smoking section. In April 2004 there was serous discussion about following the Irish and banning smoking altogether.

Detailed descriptions of restaurants appear in *The City Paper*, shorter ones in *Tallinn In Your Pocket*. A dark entrance, down poorly maintained stairs in a side street, is usually a clear indication that good food and value lies ahead. Bright lights at street level should be avoided. Exploration need no longer be limited to the Old Town; competition there is driving many new entrants to open up in the suburbs. At the time of writing, nobody has opened a revivalist Soviet restaurant, though the success of such ventures in Riga and in former East Berlin must in due course tempt some embittered members of the Russian-speaking community in Tallinn.

Most of the following restaurants have been open for several years and are popular with tourists, ex-pats and local residents. I have, however, deliberately tried to include some that are not well known abroad and which cannot afford to advertise. Apologies in advance to the many other excellent restaurants that, with more space, would also have been included. Websites are listed so that menu planning can begin abroad and not just at the table. Restaurants are on the whole very good at keeping these up to date, and for those in a rush it is possible to pre-book not only a table but also the meal. Eating in hotels is popular in Tallinn and some of their restaurants are covered in the hotel descriptions in the previous chapter.

BUDGET

Prices listed below give an indication of costs for three courses without wine. (In spring 2004, ∈1 = 15.65EEK, £1 = 23.85EEK, and US$1 = 13.00EEK.) The cost of wine varies enormously between restaurants, and is often as high as in Britain or the USA. Sticking to beer saves a lot of money – and it is, after all, an Estonian national drink. A small beer is 0.3 litres and large one is 0.5 litres. On Old Town Square and in the immediate vicinity, reckon to pay about 35EEK for a small beer and 45EEK for a large one. Elsewhere 20EEK and 30EEK are the more normal charges. Excluding drink, expect to pay about 90EEK for a two-course lunch and 250EEK for a three-course dinner.

RESTAURANTS

Balthasar Raekoja Plats 11; tel: 627 6400; web: www.restaurant.ee [2 C4]
Garlic dominates every course here, even the ice-cream, but above all in the salads. Whilst other dishes do appear on the menu, they tend to be as appetising as a vegetarian option in a steakhouse. Opening in early 2000, the restaurant took over the top floor of the former pharmacy (see page 116) and has kept as much of the original wooden furnishings as was practical. With the restaurant's views over the Town Hall Square, it is tempting to linger here

but it also offers a quiet respite over lunch between morning and afternoon sightseeing tours. The range of short drinks at the bar can be equally tempting at other times of day. 350EEK.

Bocca Olevimägi 9; tel: 641 2610; web: www.bocca.ee [2 C2]
A passer-by on the pavement here who happened to notice the plain glass windows with the two canvas panels behind them would not believe that during 2003 Bocca got more publicity abroad than all other Tallinn restaurants put together. Only the cars parked outside suggest considerable opulence inside. Critics liked the modern minimalist layout against the medieval backdrop of very solid limestone. They liked the changing lighting schemes – and the fact that plenty of modest pasta dishes were available if octopus and veal seemed unnecessarily extravagant. 400EEK.

Le Bonaparte Pikk 45; tel: 646 4444 [2 C3]
The formal restaurant at the back and the easy-going café at the front are both French through and through. The décor is very domestic and totally unpretentious. The care and flare all go into the food, which is still too rare in Tallinn, whether it is a simple cake in the café or an elaborate paté at the start of a serious meal. Other unusual touches are the individual towels in the toilets and coat-warmers for visitors in winter. Prices in both the restaurant and the café are fortunately very Estonian. 350EEK.

Controvento Katariina käik; tel: 644 0470; web: www.controvento.ee [2 D3]
Uniquely in Tallinn, this restaurant could maintain a review written when it first opened in

Restaurants

1992. It has retained the same menu, the same décor and probably many of the same clients, who want no-nonsense home cooking in an Italian bistro and no attempts to emulate temporary culinary fads. Prices have had to increase somewhat but they remain modest in comparison with the competition in the Old Town. 250EEK.

Crêperie sans Nom Müürivahe 23a; tel: 631 4336; web: www.sansnom.ee [2 D4]
The number 23a here is important: the much larger entrance for 23 makes clear its sexual offerings in Finnish. This, however, is a small French outpost with no concessions to Estonia, although it is largely Estonians rather than foreigners who come here. Some local newspapers list it in the café/bar section of their listings but this is unfair. The pancakes, both savoury and sweet, are substantial, particularly when taken with salad and then ice-cream. 200EEK.

Eeslitall (The Donkey's Stable) Dunkir 4; tel: 631 3755; web: www.eeslitall.ee [2 C4]
In the early days after independence, this restaurant was an immediate indication of changing times. Whilst its easy-going service, French sauces, enormous menus and winelists may now seem normal for Tallinn, it then set a trend which other restaurants took several years to emulate. Young and old both dine happily here (an unusual combination in Tallinn), although only the young would consider staying in the spartan hostel of the same name upstairs. The whole building closed for renovation in late 2003. 150EEK.

Eesti Maja Lauteri 1; tel: 645 5252; web: www.eestimaja.ee [1 A3]
Do not expect quick service here or even staff with much English, but instead be ready for

enormous portions and rich food at each course. It will be hard to spend more than £6/US$10 a head and many eat their fill for much less. The vegetable soup makes a good meal in itself at lunchtime. The building also houses *Global Estonian,* an English-language bi-annual magazine well worth buying for the tough interviews they give to local politicians willing to meet them. 150EEK.

Karl Friedrich Raekoja Plats 5; tel: 627 2413; web: www.restaurant.ee [2 C4]
The grand location on Town Hall Square might suggest ostentation and prices to match but fortunately this has not happened. Each floor caters for a different age-group but it is the top floor that is recommended; the long walk up and down is well worthwhile. Oldies should book well in advance for a table overlooking the square and enjoy a lingering lunch or dinner. Its fish salads are to be recommended and it has its own beer, called Karl Friedrich. 350EEK.

Klafira Vene 4; tel: 667 5144; web: www.klafira.ee [2 C4]
If Soviet Russia has been banished for good from Estonia, the Tsarist aristocracy is making an effective comeback here instead. Perhaps they were wise to wait until 2000, nine years after the re-establishment of Estonian independence, before doing so. Their food is strictly Russian, their wine is sensibly French. That rich Estonians are firstly willing to come and then secondly even to speak Russian to the staff shows the high standards the restaurant has set. Allow a full evening here and do not consider the cost beforehand. It will be expensive by Estonian standards, but not by London or New York ones. 350EEK.

Restaurants

Kuldse Notsu Kõrts (The Golden Pig) Dunkri 8; tel: 628 6567; web: www.schlossle-hotels.com [2 C4]

Although this restaurant belongs to the luxury St Petersbourg Hotel next door, the two establishments have nothing in common. This country restaurant, with low ceilings and long wooden tables, seems pleasantly incongruous in the middle of the Old Town. However, this is precisely its appeal. It offers varied Estonian fare – thick mushroom soups, pork in innumerable guises and apples in almost as many. Drink apple juice or beer rather than wine. Few tourists venture in, but many Estonians do and this must be its best recommendation. 250EEK.

Liivi Steakhouse Narva mnt 1; tel: 625 7377; web: www.steakhouse.ee [2 E3]

Everything is wonderfully predictable here, so this is the place to be unadventurous. All styles of steak are on the menu and they can be accompanied by a wide range of red wine. The starters are patés and soups and the sweets apple-pie or ice-cream. Being situated opposite the Viru Hotel in a complex that also houses the main post office, the clientele is very varied but always conventional. 300EEK.

Must Lammas (The Black Sheep) Sauna 2; tel: 644 2031; web: www.mustlammas.ee [2 D4]

For years this Georgian restaurant was called Exit but it changed its name in early 2001. Luckily little else has changed. All guests are greeted with portions of firewater and strips of salted beef as the menus are handed out. Eat meat, meat and more meat all evening, topped, if you did not have lunch, with some ice-cream drenched in brandy. Start with stuffed vine leaves and move on to beef and pork stews. Vegetarians keep out. 250EEK.

Olde Hansa Vanaturg 1; tel: 627 9020; web: www.oldehansa.com [2 C4]
Ignore the silly name and the silly costumes worn by the staff but enjoy the candles (there is no electric light) and the genuinely Estonian live music. Some tables are for two but don't venture in for a quiet, intimate evening. This is really a party venue so come as a group and with a very empty stomach. Portions are enormous, even for soup and ice-cream. 250EEK.

Peppersack Viru tänav 2; tel: 646 6900; web: www.peppersack.ee [2 C4]
Johan Peppersack was one of Tallinn's best mayors when Estonia was ruled by the Swedes in the 16th and 17th centuries. He fought the occupiers for money and for autonomy with a tenacity that no other mayor could equal in the subsequent 400 years. He would not have tolerated the mess Polish restorers, local Estonians and the Soviet occupiers got into when they tried and failed to restore the building in time for the 1980 Olympics. The compromise between Polish baroque and the former Gothic is still there. Perhaps it is better to look at the live entertainment, which can feature fencers, troubadours or martial artists. (Check the website if it matters which.) The menu is extensive but many find it easiest just to order one of the feasts at a fixed price which includes three courses and drink. 250EEK.

Teater Lai 31; tel: 646 6261 [2 B3]
Coming into this basement from the stairs will often seem like an intrusion, so glued to their cigarettes and to television are the staff and their close friends. However, walk through to a back alcove and the gathering will be interrupted to bring a mixed Creole and Estonian menu. Start with the grilled dishes from the former and finish with the pancakes from the

latter. Do not expect any tender loving care here but the cheapness and the variety of the menu will be ample compensation. 200EEK.

Toomkooli Toomkooli 13; tel: 644 6613 [3 B6]

Those who are not deterred by the awkward location at the back of the Old Town are rewarded on arrival with an extensive international menu and wine list but prices that have stayed Estonian. Minimal music and very heavy wooden chairs give a more formal air to the surroundings than is now common in many Tallinn restaurants, but in a town now so geared to the young, this should be taken as a compliment. 350EEK.

Vanaema Juures (Grandma's Place) Rataskaevu 10/12; tel: 631 3928 [2 B4]

This is probably Tallinn's most famous restaurant but not even a visit from Hillary Clinton has gone to its head. The valid and repeated descriptions of it – good home cooking, a traditional décor and a cosy atmosphere – degenerate into cliché but few would dispute them. The furnishings and photographs from the previous independence period (1918–40), together with discreet music from that time, deter the young and raucous, but others will immediately appreciate the originality of total Estonian surroundings. Unfortunately, Grandma has not got around yet to having a website. 300EEK.

CAFÉS AND BARS

There is little distinction between cafés and bars in Tallinn as no licences are needed to serve alcohol. Self-service at a counter remains common although practice varies as to whether clients then wait for the drinks or whether they are brought to the table. Those that open only in the evening are listed in the entertainment section. Those below are open all day and usually in the evening as well. Piped music is largely unavoidable but perhaps readers can help find a café where all music is banned so peace and quiet is assured. The success of those listed below should ensure that they are all around during the currency of this book, although be prepared for name changes if a new owner takes over.

Café Anglais Raekoja Plats 14; tel: 644 2160 [2 C4]
It is perhaps surprising to suggest that visitors should patronise a café always full of the ex-pat community, but the price, choice and quality of the sandwiches, salads and cakes will soon assuage any feelings of guilt, as will the view over Town Hall Square. The café is on the first floor and fortunately the darkish, austere entrance on the ground floor is hardly inviting. This tends to keep out most of the passing tourists during the summer; linger here whilst others are rushed and overcharged in the square below.

Elsebet Viru 2 [2 C4]
Lunch on the run is not yet a Tallinn phenomenon, despite the serious business environment. However, those who want to bring London practice with them can race into the ground floor here and will be out in five minutes at most with a range of sandwiches, quiches and cakes. The more sensible visitor will forget breakfast in the hotel for once to arrive here with a camera at 08.00 so that a window table on the first floor will be theirs. Stay for a couple of

Cafés and bars

hours to see the last of yesterday's drunks being picked up, the Tallinn élite coming out of their expensive flats and the first of the cruise parties meandering towards Town Hall Square. Don't forget a zoom lens to catch unsuspecting faces and Tallinn's windows and roofs.

George Browne's Harju 6 [3 D6]

This name was chosen not to commemorate Britain's notorious Foreign Secretary from the late 1960s, but after a relatively benevolent governor from the 18th century. The Brit would, however, have liked the 10.00 opening and the 01.00 closure, often extending to 02.00 at the weekend. The clientele is unusually mixed here; it is possible to drink coffee or beer, to be 20 or 60, to be Estonian or foreign. It will soon qualify for a longevity medal, having been one of the very first cafés to open in the early 1990s.

Gloria Veinikelder Müürivahe 2; web: www.gloria.ee [3 D6]

It seems a shame to ignore Estonia whilst in Tallinn but that is what anyone who comes here has to do. Forget vodka or the local Vana Tallinn and concentrate on the 2,000 different bottles not only of wine but also of cognac and whisky. Many foreigners justify their presence in this wine bar by pointing out that they can enjoy their 'own' drinks here at prices much lower than those charged at home. That the bar is called 'Napoleon' shows where most of these 2,000 bottles come from.

Kaheksa Vana-Posti 8 [3 D5]

Kaheksa means 'eight' but nobody seems to know the reason for this name. The austere granite Sõprus Cinema to which this is an adjunct is a surprising backcloth but indoors a totally tropical environment is created. The décor is light, as are the drinks, most of which are rum and coconut based. Teetotallers can hide their abstinence behind fruit-smoothies which really are light desserts. From about 2002, a Caribbean theme hit Tallinn and here it is at its best. Perhaps a visit here in midwinter is inadvisable as leaving will be a blow; wait until the summer when the outside will from time to time rival the interior.

Maiasmokk Pikk 16 [2 C3]
It is nice to find a café that is unashamedly old-fashioned. The panelling is dark, the staff middle-aged and the food prepared on the spot. It is provincial in the best sense of the word, being one of the very few cafés in Tallinn that are spared piped music. Prices also stay two or three years behind those charged elsewhere, particularly surprising given its location on the tourist beat in the centre of the Old Town. There is a separate entrance to the restaurant, which consists of small dining-rooms on the first floor that can be booked for private groups of eight to ten. Choose the view carefully: one overlooks the balcony of the Russian Embassy from which the occupation of Estonia was proclaimed in 1940. In summer 2004 the Kalev Chocolate Museum moved to the top floor of the restaurant.

McCool Suur-Karja 20; web: www.jjj-bars.com [3 D5]
As soon as it opened, this bar won the 2003 publicity stakes for several reasons. It is in the same building as the Tallinn Stock Exchange, it has one of the largest television screens and

Cafés and bars

probably the longest bar in town and it serves Chinese food. Its gimmick is that sometimes drink prices go up and down and customers need to check the television screen for bargains that may disappear for those who dither too long over their choice. Its live music programme is so varied that it needs a website to give full details. Perhaps in respect of stock market performances everywhere apart from in Tallinn, prices stayed quite reasonable throughout the year. Elder clients can take advantage of the wine bar, wisely cut off from the main bar, where relative quiet is assured.

Meistrite Hoov (Masters' Courtyard) Vene 6 [2 C4]
Whilst gentrification continues apace through most of Tallinn's Old Town, it is pleasant still to find a quarter that remains genuinely bohemian. Lavish chocolates are usually expected in boutiques or at least in department stores. Here, too, they are available, and in fact are the main attraction in a café called Chocolaterie where suits are unknown, where self-service is the norm and where soft cushions cover the chairs. Expect to be surrounded by modern art, both in painting and in ceramics. The size of the exhibition depends on the weather; it rapidly expands outdoors whenever it can.

Mini-many Maakri 22 [1 A3]
This wooden house could not be a greater contrast to the Radisson Hotel on the other side of the road. It has only five tables and serves plain home cooking on traditional black-and-white tablecloths. The clientele is largely local but the occasional foreigner is now seen here.

Mocha Vene 1 [2 C4]

Return visitors to Tallinn will remember this as the Mary and there seems little need for a name change. The selection of teas remains as extensive as that of the coffees and for those who would be happier in Austria or Germany, the Mocha provides perfect solace. After a cake or two here there is no need for lunch or supper. Papers to read abound, there is no rush and the music is much quieter than elsewhere. The neighbouring shops change frequently; let us hope that Mocha sees no need to follow suit. The Irish and Italian embassies share a building over the road so their flags plus the EU one make the café easy to find.

Otto's Pikk 35 [2 C3]

For the moment cafés are few and far between on Pikk, although it is a central street in the Old Town. Although the décor here is modern, this one generally attracts an older clientele who are rewarded with lower prices and larger portions than those usually offered elsewhere. They may also prefer the smaller size as there are only five tables.

Põllu Rävala 8 [1 A3]

The headquarters of the Estonian Civil Aviation Administration, close to the Radisson and Viru Hotels, is an unusual place to look for coffee but for those on a tight budget and not the least interested in atmosphere, the public café in the basement rewards those who track it down with coffee for 4EEK (16p/27c), light snacks for 12EEK (50p/70c) and hot meals for around 22EEK (£1/US$1.60). The hot dishes come straight from the freezer and the flowers on the tables are guaranteed to be artificial, but at these prices who should care?

Cafés and bars

Scotland Yard Mere pst 6e; tel: 653 5190 [2 E2]

Many British antique shops must have been plundfered to recreate the 1890s here, though whether gunsmiths needed to relinquish so much of their old stock is a moot point. The guns worn by the staff are fortunately fakes. Proximity to the port attracts the wilder, rougher crowd on Friday and Saturday nights, but more conventional guests will feel happy here during the day and might even want to stay for a meal.

Tristan ja Isolde Raekoja Plats 1 [2 C4]

Although part of the Town Hall, its entrance is so well concealed that, even at the height of the tourist season, space is often available. However, the most enticing time to come is in midwinter late in the evening. Stride across the deserted snow-covered square, pull open the squeaking door and enjoy *glühwein* in what looks like a Swiss country inn. Follow this with Irish coffee and chocolate cake and hopefully the warmth will last until you get back to your hotel.

Wholeword Tea Aia 4 [2 E3]

A slight misnomer as the shop really specialises in China tea and offers a full tea ceremony for those who have the time. It is part of a larger shop selling a wide range of holistic products and is the greatest contrast to any other Tallinn café a visitor is likely to find. Do not ask for the tea to be laced, do not ask for it to be served quickly and do not ask for milk. Accept these restrictions and linger over your pot for an hour or so. Therapy does not come cheaper or more congenially than it does here.

7

On regaining independence, Tallinn immediately rebelled against the limited and formal entertainment that had previously been available. Out went dance bands, string quartets and folk dancing; in came discotheques, striptease and jazz. Private enterprise immediately seized the Finnish market that came every weekend laden with money and determined to spend it – not necessarily in the most sensible of ways; vodka at a quarter of the price it is at home is bound to lead to grief. Above all, the night went on until breakfast. No club now dares to close before 02.00. Admission fees are rare so it is common to sample quite a few different places in one evening. Now that Tallinn has a large middle class, the clientele is very mixed in most clubs as Estonians no longer feel excluded from them. None are yet typecast but go for smart-casual dress. Anything torn or ill-fitting is frowned on in Estonia. Better to be out of date than out of figure.

Before the clubs open, rock and pop concerts draw large crowds to **Linnahall**, near the harbour. It has performances most evenings.

Only opera and ballet have stayed unscathed since 1990, with a regular classical repertoire sung in the original language. The 2003–04 season, for instance, is offering *Carmen*, *Coppelia*, *Don Giovanni* and *The Merry Widow*, but only one opera by a contemporary Estonian composer. It is now a struggle to finance these performances but luckily the money is always found.

OPERA AND CONCERTS

The **Estonian National Opera** [1 A3] (web: www.opera.ee) has performances three or four times a week. Specialist tour operators can pre-book tickets as the programme is fixed about six months in advance. Given the inevitable government cutbacks in this field, it is remarkable how up to date the building now is following its 1998 reconstruction, with the stage lighting being particularly impressive. Unlike Riga, Estonia's opera rarely attracts world-famous performers – and indeed some Estonian performers, especially in this field, have been attracted abroad by the much higher fees paid there. The fact that about 30% of the opera's tickets year-round are sold to non-Estonians shows the high standard that it offers, as well as the very reasonable prices charged. Performances are always in the original language; 20% or so are of contemporary Estonian works, the remainder are popular classics. The opera is closed in July and August.

Classical concerts are held in the **Old Town Hall** [2 C4], the **Estonia Concert Hall** [1 A3], the **House of Blackheads** [2 C3] and in **St Nicholas' Church** [3 C5], all of these venues being in the Old Town. In most cases tickets are sold only on the day or the day before the concert so there is no need (or possibility) to pre-book from abroad. Whilst some performances take place in midsummer, music-lovers are well advised to come at other times of year when the choice and standard is far higher.

Young people congregate at **Linnahall** [1 A1], the concert hall beside the heliport near the harbour, where live music is staged most evenings. Performers are always local. Sometimes this is replaced by family shows and sometimes by raucous Russian plays not genteel enough for the main Russian Theatre. The website www.linnahall.ee is only in Estonian (*Pileti hind* are the ticket prices and *Jäähalli* is the ice-skating rink).

Films are always subtitled and never dubbed so tourists can see films missed at home without any problem. The **Sõprus** Cinema (web: www.kino.ee) in the Old Town at Vana-Posti 8 [3 D5] is easily accessible from many hotels. Younger people now flock to **Coca-Cola Plaza** [2 E3] (web: www.superkinod.ee), a combination of 11 separate cinemas and a shopping mall. It is situated behind the Central Post Office on Viru Square and so is also close to many hotels.

NIGHTLIFE

Tallinn prides itself on its nightlife and some tour operators promote it extensively. It does tend to attract some people who should really have kept their vomiting and urinating back home in Britain and Finland. As a major stag destination in 2003, perhaps it will fall from popularity in 2004 when these crowds move elsewhere.

Fortunately, nightclubs do not go in and out of favour as quickly in Tallinn as they do elsewhere and many clubs that were thriving six or seven years ago still do so now. Many do not charge an entrance fee, particularly midweek, so if you find you have stumbled into somewhere not to your taste, it won't cost much to move on.

The clubs listed below are all totally different, and this is deliberate. *Tallinn In Your Pocket* keeps very up to date on this topic as it is published six times a year and not being dependent on advertising can be objective. To whet your appetite, check their website, www.inyourpocket.com, before leaving home.

Nightlife

Bonnie & Clyde Olümpia Hotel, Liivalaia 33 [1 A3]

As this club is safely ensconced in a four-star hotel, it is never a mistake to suggest a date here. Do, however, dress up properly, firstly to get in and secondly not to lower the tone. If you are under 25, you may well not want to try unless you can be sure of being taken for at least 30.

Eiffel Grand Hotel, Toompuiestee 27 [3 A7]

The hotel caters for staid, elderly tourist groups wanting a quiet base near the Old Town, but this rooftop club is far more broad-minded, both in its music and in its clientele. The music is normally live, which makes the volume sensible for those wanting to be able to talk with their guests. The view up to the floodlit Tall Hermann Tower is a pleasant contrast to the cellar walls on offer in so many other clubs, as is the space to move around. Smart-casual dress is the norm, though extremes in either direction can sometimes be seen.

Harley Davidson Dunkri 11 [2 C4]

This club must clearly be a rebellion against the deluxe St Petersbourg Hotel on the other side of the road. Nobody here has any dress sense at all and if they cannot arrive on a motorbike, will certainly not choose a taxi instead. Pretend to be under 25 to be comfortable here and, yes, a leather jacket is the common currency. Probably to stop endless protests from hotel grandees, the club closes at midnight during the week and at the comparatively early time of 02.00 on Friday and Saturday nights.

La Casa del Habano Dunkri 2 [2 C4]

For those who hate nightlife but for business reasons have to pretend otherwise, Tallinn's first cigar lounge provided the perfect answer. To impress, insist on a Cuban cigar, but the miserly can also order Danish and Dutch ones. Sit at the window during the evening and see all of single Tallinn go by, some to the deluxe St Petersbourg Hotel and some to the Harley Davidson described above. As the lounge is also open during the day, come back then for a different view of families and cruise passengers.

Molly Malone's Mündi 2 [2 C4]

Yes, the old aluminium Guinness advertisements are corny, yes the music can be dated and yes, because of the location on Town Hall Square it can get very crowded in summer, but nonetheless a visit to Tallinn is not complete without a look-in here. Ex-pats regularly congregated here, even before fish and chips came on to the menu. In the summer, spilling on to the square is normal so relative peace can alternate with Irish liveliness.

GAY TALLINN

Given Tallinn's devotion to anything Western, it is rather surprising how limited the gay scene is. Whilst the legal restraints they faced in Soviet times have all of course been abolished, the hostility the gay community then faced has still not been eradicated. As a result, open affection outside the few gay clubs is very unusual and visitors are advised to avoid this. Some clubs even function behind closed doors and it is necessary to ring a bell to gain admission. Opening hours can often change, as can nights on which women are admitted. This should be checked on their websites. Three well-established clubs are:

Nightman Vineeri 4; web: www.nightman.ee
This club just southwest of the Old Town off Liivalaia started as one strictly for gays but now both straights and gays happily mix here. It makes no effort to attract foreigners – its website is still only in Estonian – and it opens only on Friday and Saturday, but nonetheless consistently fills up, so arrive on the dot of 22.00 or wait until around 03.00 to be sure of admission.

Ring Club Juhkentali 11; web: www.ringclub.ee [1 B4]
Women and striptease are strictly segregated here but do check the explicit and detailed English-language website before setting off. Juhkentali is close to the bus station and is hardly the most salubrious road in Tallinn, which perhaps suits the risqué approach of this club and the gloomy underground surroundings in which its activities take place.

X-Baar Sauna 1; web: www.zone.ee/xbaar [2 D4]
With its central location, comparatively long history and small size, this is probably the place to go first in Tallinn. The jazz and the pink décor will provide reassuring surroundings.

8

From Monday to Friday most shops open 10.00–18.00 and on Saturday they close earlier, usually around 16.00. On Sunday they stay closed. However, those in the Old Town of interest to tourists open in the summer 10.00–19.00 seven days a week. Supermarkets open seven days a week, usually 09.00–21.00. It is now rare to find a shop that does not accept credit cards although they are not, of course, of use in the markets. There is one all-night shop in the Old Town, Kolm Jalg at Pikk 3 [2 C4], and another just outside it, Westmani at Pärnu 19 [1 A3].

BOOKS AND POSTCARDS

Apollo Viru 23; web: www.apollo.ee [2 E4]

This is Tallinn's first book and map shop that's geared to the ex-pat community and the tourists walking past from the harbour into the Old Town. The windows have an extensive display of tourist literature, everything is labelled in English and there is a café. It also stocks maps and guides to the surrounding Baltic countries. Perhaps wisely, it has closed the ramshackle antiquarian section that used to be attached. If you have run out of reading matter, this is the place to stock up. English-language paperbacks cost roughly the same as in the UK.

Felix and Fabian Harju 1, just below St Nicholas' Church [3 D5]

Always stocks a wide selection of picture books, guidebooks and postcards. These names are well known in Estonia as Felix is the leading character in a novel by Friedebert Tuglas (1886–1971) and Fabian appears often in the books of Mihkel Mutt (born 1953) so this name combines two different periods of Estonian literature.

Huma Vene 14; web: www.huma.ee [2 C3]

Publishes many of the postcards sold around the Old Town as well as some of the booklets and calendars, so anyone willing to climb to their third floor office will be rewarded with lower prices than those on the street.

Juhan Hammer Voorimehe 9; web: www.oldbooks.ee [2 B4]

This is the least disorganised of Tallinn's many second-hand bookshops for those who succeed in finding it open. Most foreigners come here to find something unexpected from home, rather than anything on Estonia, but the collection of old Estonian postcards is always thorough.

Raamatukoi Viru 21; web: www.raamatukoi.ee [2 E4]

Has the most surprising entrance of any bookshop in Tallinn, as it is on the first floor and the ground floor houses a beautician with about 200 different lipsticks. The trip upstairs is worthwhile for both current books and for the choice of English-language booklets printed early in the 1990s or towards the end of the Soviet period when Moscow's political grip was loosening.

Rahva Raamat Pärnu mnt 10 [1 A3]

Probably Tallinn's most famous bookshop. Its extensive second-hand section is a treasure-trove of works on art and architecture, many totally in English or with at least an English summary in it. The premises became 'threatened' by Hugo Boss in autumn 2003 who were eager to purchase some of the current shop as an outlet for their clothes and could of course offer a much higher rent than a bookshop could pay. The wave of protests to which this gave rise, led by Estonia's most famous writer Jaan Kross, was not in the end successful and visitors in 2004 will see a much smaller bookshop here as a result.

SOUVENIRS

A one-stop shop for souvenirs, since it stocks linen, woollen jerseys, ceramics, and wooden toys, is **Puupood** at Lai 5 [2 B4]. Although in the Old Town, it is just off the main tourist circuit so prices are very reasonable.

A walk along **Katariina Käik** between Vene and Müürivahe [2 D3] will satisfy even the most fastidious shopper. This lane is lined with workshops covering every form of applied art, so tourists with time can order an item of clothing or jewellery specifically to their taste. Turn right into Müürivahe for the **Wall of Sweaters** [2 D3]. Whether the temperature is 30°F or 30°C, the stock here is always the same, geared totally to the needs of an Estonian winter. By also buying socks, gloves and fur hats, visitors are granted complete protection against it.

Helina Tilk, Rataskaevu 6 [2 B4], has probably the largest selection of locally produced china and glassware. Very little of their work has pictures of Tallinn on it since the aim is to represent local art, not to provide mantelpiece dust collectors.

For those who can restrict themselves to wooden dolls, **Nukupood** on Town Hall Square (Raekoja Plats 18) [2 C4] is conveniently located and has an enormous choice.

Kaubamaja is Tallinn's largest department store and is situated halfway between the Viru and Radisson Hotels at Gonsiori 2 [1 A3]. It will supply any forgotten toiletry article or item of clothing and is worth visiting for its CDs of Estonian music and for its porcelain. Take the outside lift to look down on the redevelopment of Viru Square. **Stockmann** is the department store where all successful Estonians like to be seen doing their shopping. It is a branch of Helsinki's most famous department store. One outlet is attached to the Viru Hotel [1 A3] and the main shop is next to the Olümpia Hotel, at Liivalaia 53 [1 A3].

In midsummer an arts and crafts market stretches across **Raekoja Plats** (Town Hall Square) [2 C4]. Do, however, watch out for pickpockets here since this is their favourite haunt. To see where local people not yet seduced by supermarkets do their daily shopping, visit **Keskturg** (Central Market), ironically only about 200m from Stockmann, just off the Tartu Road [1 B3]. Do not expect any of the elegance of Riga market here; it in fact only got a roof in 2003 so down to earth is probably the best description of it, particularly as much of the trade is in fruit and vegetables. Some Finns come for spare parts for their cars, basic linen goods and pirate CDs.

FOOD AND DRINK

As Estonia's entry into the European Union will allow visitors from other member states to bring home virtually all the drink and tobacco they can take in their luggage, it is worthwhile looking around at the prices different shops charge for these goods. Avoid the ones by the harbour as they are frequented by desperate Finns who will pay anything as long as it is less than in Helsinki. Buy the local vodka and the aperitif Vana Tallinn as savings will be greater here than on imported goods.

The **Rimi** supermarket at Aia 7 [2 D3], which is open seven days a week from 09.00 to 21.00, is the best source of picnic supplies and provisions for self-caterers. Nowhere is the demise of the USSR clearer than here as the selection is mostly American rather than European. The provision of free coffee by the cakes counter is a clever marketing device to ensure visitors linger longer and buy more. The shop also has an extensive soft and alcoholic drinks section.

Also in Aia, at 5b next to the Tavid foreign exchange bureau, is **Bakhos** [2 D3], open daily 08.00–21.00, which is one of the cheapest sources of drink in Tallinn. **Araxis** [1 A3] in the Old Fire Station on Viru Square is another popular source for drink, partly because it is open 24 hours a day. **Ararat** [1 A3], next to the bookshop Apollo in Viru, also opens 24 hours.

Cigarettes are best bought by the carton rather than by the packet. Costs vary quite considerably from kiosk to kiosk so it is worth looking around outside the Old Town where prices are invariably lower than within it.

Kalev, Estonia's famous chocolate producer, has a shop at Lai 1 [2 B4] in the centre of the Old Town but chocoholics should also check the new location of their museum above Maiasmokk café at Pikk 16 [2 C3].

Food and drink

9

Tourists tend to concentrate on the Old Town but many modern buildings are of interest too. While the main sights in the Old Town can be covered in one day, more time is needed for other sights. A route for a day-long walking tour is suggested followed by some other shorter ones.

THE WALK

Start at the final Soviet architectural legacy to Estonia, the **National Library** (Eesti Rahvusraamatukogu), begun in 1986 and completed in 1993 (page 112 [3 C8]). It is situated on the intersection of Endla and Tõnismägi close to the Mihkli and Santa Barbara hotels.

Cross the road to **St Charles's Church** (Kaarlikirik). With its almost Episcopalian simplicity it is the perfect antidote to what is to come later in the walk (page 119 [3 C8]). On leaving the church, turn right into Kaarli and then take the first road on the left, Toompea. The **Occupation Museum** opened here in summer 2003 (page 114 [3 C7]).

Continuing up the hill, at the first crossroads, note the simple monument to August 20 1991, the date Estonia declared independence during the failed Moscow coup. Had it been necessary, Estonians were ready to use the walls and towers to defend the Old Town from possible Soviet attack but the quick collapse of the coup and the immediate recognition by the USSR of Estonian independence prevented this. Looking ahead is a monument that dates from the 15th century, **Pikk Hermann** (Tall Hermann Tower [3 B6]). It has withstood numerous invasions and remains intact. Its height of nearly 50m is supported by foundations 15m deep. The first Estonian flag was flown from here in 1884, 34 years before the country was to become independent. Subsequent conquerors always marked their success by raising a flag here. A German guidebook printed in 1942 lists 12 major dates in Tallinn's history, the last being August 28 1941, when the German flag was raised over Pikk Hermann. During the Soviet occupation, the Estonian SSR flag was flown, but the Estonian national flag returned in 1989. It is raised at sunrise and lowered at sunset, except at midsummer when it is not lowered at all on the night of June 23/24. The blue in the flag represents the sky, black the soil, and white the aspirations of the Estonian people.

Tall Hermann Tower

Turn right down the hill (Komandandi) to **Kiek in de Kök** ('Peep in the Kitchen', page 111 [3 C6]). The reason for the name becomes obvious as one climbs the 45m tower to the sixth floor and peers into more and more houses; only the steeples of St Nicholas and St Olav are higher. Kiek in de Kök does not have any catering but the nearest tower to it, **Megedi**, can be recommended in this respect. This tower, like most in the city wall, dates from the late 14th century and was continually enlarged during the 15th century. From around 1800 when its defensive potential declined, it was converted

The walk

into a barracks. In 1980 the top floor became a café which uses the name Megedi, and the ground floor a restaurant, called Neitsitorn.

On leaving Kiek in de Kök turn back up the hill and turn right into Toompea, which ends in the square between **Parliament** (Riigikogu, page 115 [3 B6]) and the **Alexander Nevsky Cathedral** (page 119 [3 B6]). The juxtaposition of these two buildings appropriately contrasts official Estonian and Russian architecture. The one is simple, small and functional, the other elaborate and deliberately powerful, a completely Russian architectural outpost dominating the Tallinn skyline. The **Parliament Building**, most of which dates from 1921, is one of very few in the Old Town to have seen frequent reconstruction, the last one resulting from a fire in 1917 which may have been started by the Bolsheviks.

Toompea

Continue up the hill along Toomkooli with the post office on your right. By the end of 2004, this street should be completely restored, the first one to be back to its 1920s' glory. Straight ahead, on Kiriku Square, is the **Dome Church** (Toomkirik), sometimes called St Mary's Cathedral (page 120 [3 B5]).

As you turn left out of the church, the **Estonian Art Museum** (page 107 [3 B5]) dominates the opposite side of Kiriku Square. Turning sharp right from the museum along Toom Rüütli leads, after 150m, to the main viewpoint across Tallinn. It is inevitably crowded during the tourist season so an alternative can be recommended along Rahukohtu, on the corner of Rüütli. Rahukohtu also starts on the right-hand side of the gallery. To reach the lower town, it is necessary in either case to return along Piiskopi towards the Russian cathedral and then to walk down the steps of Lühike Jalg ('Short Leg'), rather a misnomer as there are in fact about 100 steps. At the top, though, are several tempting cafés, souvenir shops and well-maintained toilets which can provide a respite before continuing the walk. Before starting the descent, look to the left along Pikk Jalg ('Long Leg'). The façade which commands one of the best views over Tallinn is modelled on the main building of Tartu University. Perhaps appropriately, in view of the current strength of the Estonian economy, this imposing building houses the Ministry of Finance. On the right at the end of Lühike Jalg is the **Adamson-Eric Museum** (page 103 [3 C5]).

Continuing down the hill, the steps become a road which continues to a junction. To the left is Rataskaevu and to the right, Rüütli, both roads which house some of Tallinn's most famous restaurants. Ahead is **Niguliste** (St Nicholas' Church, page 122 [3 C5]), unusual in Tallinn in having been a military installation as well as a church, with ample hiding places and secret exits to the city walls. Coming out of the church and turning left along Rüütli, the next building on the left is the Swedish **Church of St Michael** (page 122 [3 C5]).

The walk

On leaving the church, turn right to the memorial to the writer **Eduard Vilde** (1865–1933). The illustrations depict scenes from his novels and plays, and the two stones represent an open book. Between 1918 and 1920 he served as Estonian Ambassador in Copenhagen and Berlin, convincing both governments that an independent Estonia was here to stay. The **Tallinn Tourist Information Centre** [3 C5] is on the other side of the road. Proceed down the steps to Harju. Ahead is the bookshop Felix & Fabian, but on the corner of Harju and Kuninga note the plaque to the writer Juhan Smuul (1922–1971) who lived here as the building belongs to the writers union. Despite winning both Stalin and Lenin prizes and being chairman of the Writers Union, he was a genuinely popular writer at the time which is why the plaque has not been removed. Hopefully, his works will soon be republished. Jaan Kross (born 1920), Estonia's most famous contemporary writer, still lives in this complex and is fit enough to reach his fourth-floor flat without a lift. (In Soviet times, only buildings with five floors or more had lifts installed.)

Turn into Harju. The bombed site on the right has deliberately been left as it was, following the bombing raid of March 9 1944. The inscription commemorates the 463 people killed that night. In June 2002 a referendum was held in Tallinn about the future of this site. Only 2% of the population turned out to vote, but 87% of them wanted to keep the site as a memorial and not let it fall into the hands of developers. Returning along Harju and then Kullassepa brings one into **Raekoja Plats**, or Town Hall Square [2 C4]. Just before reaching the square, it is worth turning right for a few minutes into the small alley, Raekoja. The building on the right, which now houses the **Photographic Museum** (page 116 [2 C4]), was the town's main prison until the early 19th century.

The Town Hall Square is similar to many in northern Germany as it was the commercial centre for the Baltic Germans. In the 16th century, the Germans accounted for about 1,500 of Tallinn's total population of around 5,000. They maintained all positions of authority, ruling from the Town Hall and the surrounding buildings. The square was the centre for all major events in the town, happy and tragic. Carnivals, weddings and Christmas have all been regularly celebrated here and the Tallinn Old Days Festival, held each year in early June, recreates the carnival atmosphere with its musical and artistic events. What was probably the world's first Christmas tree was displayed here in 1441. Yet the square was also the site for frequent executions and floggings, its grimmest day being in 1806 when 72 peasants were executed following a failed uprising. Nowadays it is hard to imagine such a background as work and punishment have given way to total relaxation. Cafés surround the square and spread into it during the summer. From 2001, a Christmas market has taken place here throughout December. One of the few buildings on the square that has kept its original function is the **Pharmacy** (page 116 [2 C4]), which dates from 1422. The **Town Hall** (page 117

Town Hall

The walk

[2 C4]) is the only late Gothic building still intact in Estonia, dating largely from the 15th century.

Across the square, opposite the Town Hall, are several short streets which lead to Pikk. On the corner of Mündi and Town Hall Square is a millennium clock which counted down the seconds until midnight on December 31 1999. Saiakäik is the smallest street in Tallinn. Take either Mündi or Saiakäik and turn right to the junction of Pikk and Pühavaimu for the **Holy Ghost Church** (Pühavaimu, page 121 [2 C4]). Cross Pikk for the **Estonian History Museum** (Ajaloomuuseum, page 108 [2 C4]), whose building is as impressive as any of the contents, perhaps more so. As you turn left into Pikk, the new Russian Embassy is on the left and on the right is Maiasmokk [2 C3], a café that has deliberately stayed old-fashioned both in décor and in prices. The name translates appropriately as 'sweet tooth'. In summer 2004 the **Kalev Chocolate Museum** moved here too (page 109 [2 C3]). Pikk has two of the few notable Jugendstil or art nouveau buildings in Tallinn, both designed by Jacques Rosenbaum. Number 18, next to Maiasmokk, has a flamboyant Egyptian theme; number 25 on the corner of Hobusepea is more modest. Number 61, built across Pagari, and probably the blandest building in the Old Town, was the KGB headquarters in Soviet times and now houses the Interior Ministry. Unlike its opposite number in Vilnius, it has not been opened to the public.

Next on the left is **St Olav's Church** (Oleviste, page 124 [2 C2]), named after the king of Norway and now a Baptist church. A few yards further down on the right is **Fat Margaret's Tower** (page 93 [2 C1]) which houses the **Maritime Museum** (Meremuuseum, page 112 [2 C1]). Outside is a plaque unveiled by Prince Andrew in May 1998 which commemorates British naval involvement in the battles between Estonian forces and the Bolsheviks from 1918 to 1920.

Turn right out of the museum and leave the Old Town on Suur Rannavärara, the continuation of Pikk. On the right is the monument to those who died in the *Estonia* tragedy in 1994. It can be interpreted in a number of ways, perhaps symbolising the boat breaking into two or the total divide between life and death. Cross Põhja puiestee to the disused power station, now ironically the **Energy Museum** (Energeetikamuuseum, page 106 [2 C1]). Built originally in the late 1920s, it then had some claim to Jugendstil influence but many subsequent alterations have completely removed any hint of beauty and style.

Return into the Old Town and walk behind Fat Margaret along Uus. Number 37 is the **Marine Mine Museum** (page 93 [2 C2]) which opened in 2003. The mines displayed here (and the objects made out of them) all come from Naissaar Island (page 141 [2 C2]) off the coast from Tallinn, which was the centre of production for the whole of the Soviet Union. Number 31 is the **Scottish Club** [2 C2], in fact a restaurant open to all. It has the best-maintained lawn in Estonia. Next door is a whisky shop, a clear testimony to Tallinn's affluence and passion for Western consumer goods. It is hard to believe that until 1989 whisky was available only in foreign currency shops. Turn right into Olevimägi and then left into Vene. On the left is a smaller, but no less Russian version of the Alexander Nevsky Cathedral, **St**

Nicholas' Russian Orthodox Church [2 C3]. Again no concessions are made to Estonia; everything is written, spoken and sung in Russian. It dates from the early 19th century. On the right at number 17 is the **City Museum** (Linnamuuseum, page 105 [2 C3]). As with the History Museum, the building is as of much interest as the contents. Having escaped the fires that ravished so many buildings in the Old Town, this 14th-century merchant's house still has examples of 16th-century wooden panelling, windows and furniture.

On the right are the ruins of the **Dominican Monastery** [2 D3], founded in 1246 but destroyed during the Reformation in 1524 when the monks were forced to flee. Extensive archaeological excavations were carried out between 1954 and 1968 when the ruins were first opened to the public. Take a torch and wear sturdy shoes as the surviving ambulatories are poorly lit. Of most interest are the stone carvings by the 16th-century Dutch sculptor Arent Passer. Chamber-music concerts take place here during the summer. On leaving the monastery, turn left into Vene and left again into **Katariina Käik** [2 D3]. Gravestones from the monastery are lined up along the left-hand wall. This tiny alleyway is where local ex-pats buy their souvenirs of Tallinn, as few tourists find it. It is also used as a film-set. Turn right at the end into Müürivahe, which runs below the city walls. Elderly Russians have stalls here, selling woollen sweaters, gloves and socks both in midsummer and in midwinter. The walk ends at the junction with Viru Street. To the left is the 15th-century **Viru Gate** [2 E3], as formidable as the fortifications seen at the start of the walk. To the right is McDonald's; will it also last five centuries?

Visitors with more time can see many museums in addition to those mentioned in the walk. Close to the Viru Gate at Vana Viru 14 and opposite the Viru Hotel is the **Fire-Fighting Museum** (page 108 [2 E3]). Back in the Old Town, in Lai, are the **Applied Arts Museum** (page 104 [2 B4]) at number 17 and the **Health Museum** (page 109 [2 B3]) at numbers 28–30.

Next to the Applied Arts Museum is the **Natural History Museum** (page 114 [2 B4]) at Lai 29, and then the **Theatre and Music Museum** (page 117 [3 D5]) at Müürivahe 12. Just outside the Old Town, behind the railway station at Kotzebue 16, is the **Dolls' Museum** (page 106 [2 A2]).

FURTHER WALKS
From the Radisson Hotel

Tourists staying at the Radisson Hotel [1 A3] tend to walk directly through the Viru Gate into the Old Town but if they briefly turn in the other direction they will be well rewarded. Archaeological remains are being discovered on **Vaike Pääsukese**, close to the Radisson Hotel, which probably date back to the 13th century. Panels above the site beside the glass roof give the current picture and with prior arrangement it is possible to go on to the site. Some wooden buildings remain on **Maakri** as an incongruous contrast to the increasing number of skyscrapers that surround them. Note in particular number 23, built in 1910 as a textile workshop and restored in 1996. The road sign at the corner of Maakri and Tornimäe is probably unique for central Tallinn. It is still bilingual in Russian and

Further walks

Estonian. One of the first acts of the government after the restoration of independence in 1991 was to remove Russian completely from all public places and most such street signs had been replaced, or at least had the Russian whitewashed over, by the end of 1992. The **Armenian Church** at Tartu 16a also looks increasingly out of place in this ultra-mercenary environment. The building was for most of its life a Catholic church but the local Armenian community took it over in 1994. Note the lack of icons inside, which distinguishes their religious practices so clearly from those of the Russian Orthodox community.

20th-century Tallinn

A walk from the Viru Gate [2 E3] along either Pärnu mnt or Estonia pst, and then along Kaarli pst back to the **National Library** [3 C8], passes the main buildings that remain from the end of the Tsarist period and the first independence period, ie: from 1900 until 1940. Jugendstil, neo-classicism and functionalism are all represented here and it is to be hoped that developers do not get permission to make drastic changes. At present the only likely change is thought to be at the Sakala Conference Centre, in fact a Soviet building, which if rebuilt could compete with the more modern facilities in the larger hotels.

The **Estonian National Theatre** [3 E5] was designed by a Finnish architect, Armas Lindgren, and opened in 1913, although the rebuilding that followed the bombing of Tallinn in 1944 was carried out under the Estonian architect Alar Kotli. The money for the original building was raised by private subscription and the

Tsarist authorities attempted to block the project. They did briefly succeed in preventing the Estonian language from being used in any production. In 1918 The Estonian National Assembly met here.

On the opposite side of Estonia pst from the theatre is the **Estonian Bank Museum** (page 108 [3 E6]) which was modernised in the summer of 1998. The **Sakala Conference Centre** [3 E6], a Soviet-era building behind the Bank Museum, is best known for the stained glass of Rait Prääts whose work can also be seen in St Nicholas Church and in the National Library. It is thought that this area is likely to be developed soon with many office and hotel projects now under consideration.

On **Vabaduse Väljak** (Freedom Square [3 D6]), the Palace Hotel and the Town Hall beside it both date from the 1930s. Their size and the imposing nature of similar buildings along Pärnu mnt testify to the confidence of the regime at the time. Behind them are a number of functionalist buildings that survived the 1944 bombing raid. A statue of Peter the Great was erected in the square in 1910 to commemorate the 200th anniversary of the surrender of Tallinn by the Swedes to the Russians. It was removed only in 1923, several years after independence. Pictures of parades there before 1923 show Peter the Great looking down on the Estonian president. Nobody knows what happened to the top of the statue, but the metal from the base was used to mint Estonian coins. The Soviets had their parades here (when it was called Victory Square) and now each February 24, which is National Day, there is a march past in front of the president and the

Further walks

TALLINN IN 1938
Ronald Seth, extract from 'Baltic Corner'

In the middle of Tallinn is a large asphalted space called Freedom Square. If an ugly white Lutheran church standing to one side of it were removed, it would be a much finer square than it is already. On two sides it is open, on the other two are modern buildings in the latest, yet simple, modern style. If you stand in the middle of the square – not to be recommended now that they have taken the flower-bed away – facing the double avenue of trees leading up to another church with twin spires, you will have on your left an immense building in reddy-brown glazed brick, the property of an insurance company. If you look at it close to, I think you will agree with me that it is a very ugly building. Its height and the luxury of its interior appointments, however, are impressive, and on its ground floor was the 'Corso', one of the favourite coffee-house rendezvous, where as much business was done as in a great many offices; perhaps more. The 'Corso' unfortunately is no more, and its clientele has transferred to other newer coffee-houses.

prime minister. It is sad that much of this square, so important in Estonian history, is now a car park. At least the layout improved somewhat in December 2003 when the **Freedom Clock** was unveiled. This consists in fact of two

If you face this building, the EKA, on its left you will see the 'Gloria Palace', erected by a Jew, and though of simple exterior appearance it is typically flamboyant, all gilt and glittering glass inside. In the basement is a bar and restaurant with one of the best dance floors in Tallinn. To the left of the 'Gloria' is the new Palace Hotel, not quite as high as the EKA, but high enough to be impressive and again built in good simple taste.

Now turn about, and the buildings you see on this side are no less impressive. On the right are the National Art Galleries which we used to admire until the huge Eeks Maja building beside it was finished, which now makes it look rather miniature. This new house, built by the Houseowners Bank, is as high as EKA but much more attractive and, for me, more impressive, with floor upon floor of really exclusive flats and offices and modern shops beneath. Freedom Square is representative of modern Estonian architectural aspirations. Here, right in the middle of a city where ancient and modern buildings have sprung side by side with a deliberate inconsiderateness, it seems to me that in no way are these buildings covering up or spoiling the old medieval treasures.

towers, one in limestone with a traditional clock and one in steel with two digital timers marking the time from the first declaration of independence in February 1918 and then from the end of Soviet power in August 1991.

Changing Tallinn

A walk again from Viru Gate across Viru Square [2 E3] gives an appropriately unflattering picture of the construction that took place between 1960 and 1980 but a more positive one of what happened between 2002 and 2004. Looking back towards Narva mnt, the **Viru Hotel** [1 A3] is a major eyesore and the inevitable result of conflicting Soviet policies in the early 1970s. On the one hand, tourists needed to be admitted to Tallinn to boost the country's international image; on the other, they must not be allowed serious contact with the local population. An isolated tower block was obviously the answer and until 1980, when some of the Olympic Games were held in Tallinn, the Viru was the only hotel for foreigners. Many probably saw Tallinn only from the bar on the 22nd floor. Estonians console themselves with the knowledge that the Viru Hotel did at least spare them a 'Stalinist cathedral' which was one proposal for this location; an enormous memorial to Mikhail Kalinin was another idea. Kalinin, a member of Lenin's Politburo, lived in Tallinn for three years between 1901 and 1904 whilst he was banished from St Petersburg. A Soviet guidebook published in 1987 blames the lack of 'artistic and economic means' for the failure of both projects. One published a year or two later might have given the true reason: the intense local opposition. A more modest statue of Kalinin was instead erected on Tower Square, a park between the Old Town and the railway station. (As with most other Soviet statues, it was removed in the early 1990s.)

Behind the Viru Hotel is the **Kaubamaja** department store, built in the 1960s but modernised on many occasions since. In the Soviet period it was crudely divided between a shop for the local population and one for foreigners. Both were flagships in their different ways. The local shop was better supplied than most in St Petersburg and Moscow and the notorious 'Berioshka', which took only precious *valuta* (hard foreign currencies) in exchange for vodka, wooden dolls and fur hats, was the only Soviet shop that thousands of tourists would ever enter. In the 1990s Viru Square was a dismal muddle of kiosks, bus stops and car parks. In 2002 and 2003 it was a building site but by April 2004 it had been completely transformed into a modern shopping centre with an extended Viru Hotel on one side and the Tallink Hotel on the other.

Before the war, the main Tallinn synagogue existed on this site where Kaubamaja now stands. The current **synagogue** [1 B2] shares premises with the Jewish School on Karu, near the harbour, and was opened in December 2000. It is the only active synagogue in Estonia and replaced a temporary building used in Soviet times on Magdaleena Street in the southern part of the city. Sadly, the occasional brutal attack on the premises has meant that they carry no outside identification. The building is now the headquarters for the small Jewish community in Tallinn. Visitors, both Jewish and non-Jewish, are welcome to visit the synagogue.

Returning towards town, Karu becomes Ahtri which skirts the harbour. Now very dwarfed by the huge boats that ply between Helsinki and Tallinn, the icebreaker *Suur Tõll* still stands out as a boat clearly moored here for a long stay. Having been delivered to the Tsarist navy in 1914 from the Stettin shipyards in Germany, it would inevitably have a complicated history over the next eight years, being based in Tallinn all that time. The Finns and Estonians who operated it wanted to prevent its fall into either White Russian or Bolshevik hands and, under the Tartu Treaty signed between the USSR and Estonia in February 1920, it was finally given to the Estonians. It could break ice a metre thick when launched and it was still doing so with the same equipment in the late 1980s. Visitors can see the engines, the living quarters and the two separate kitchens from which food for the officers and for the men was prepared. It is possible that the boat will be moved during 2004. Check its website www.aktivist.ee/suurtoll for the current state of play.

Walking tours

10

MUSEUMS

Most museums close at least one day a week – usually Monday or Tuesday – and some for two days; they also close on public holidays. Many do not open until 11.00 and only one, the Architecture Museum, stays open until 20.00. Churches are open every day from around 09.00.

Admission prices given here are for adults. Most museums give reductions for children and for senior citizens. There is no charge on February 18 (International Guides Day) and May 18 (International Museums Day) for many of the museums listed. Several state museums share the website www.ekm.ee, and several city ones www.linnamuuseum.ee.

Adamson-Eric Museum Lühike Jalg 3; tel: 644 5838; web: www.ekm.ee [3 C5] Open Wed–Sun 11.00–18.00 Admission 10EEK

Adamson-Eric (1902–68) was without doubt the most famous Estonian artist who worked during both the independence period and the Soviet era. This house has no links with him, although before being used as a museum it did have workshops for coppersmiths. The museum opened in 1983 and the collection is based on around 1,000 works bequeathed by his widow. These cover his whole life in both painting and applied art. Gifts from abroad have recently been added to the collection. Labels are in English. Adamson-Eric's parents were able to pay for long periods of study during the 1920s in both Paris and Berlin. Elements of Fauvism and Cubism can be seen in many of his pictures but he was equally drawn to the Bauhaus and worked closely with Walter Gropius, George Grosz and Otto Dix. On his return to Estonia he first specialised in portraits, then added landscapes and broadened into applied arts. In this field, his work became as diverse as his painting. Around 1930 he began with tapestries and textiles and then added ceramics and metalwork to his range. Shortly before the war he diversified even more, starting to work with leather and to design stage sets. He retreated with the Soviet army in 1941 and managed to maintain his artistic integrity despite the stringent demands of Soviet officialdom. With the inevitable lack of materials for applied art at this time, he concentrated again on painting. In 1949, the political tide finally turned against him and he was expelled from the Communist Party, forced to give up his posts and sent into factory work. Although released in 1953 on Stalin's death, his health had deteriorated and he suffered a stroke in 1955. His reaction was simply to learn to paint as well with his left hand as he had previously done with his right! His health slowly improved and he was able to add porcelain painting and tile design to his work in the field of applied art. He remained active until shortly before his death in 1968.

Applied Arts Museum Lai 17; tel: 641 1927; web: www.ekm.ee [2 B3] Open Wed–Sun 11.00–18.00 Admission 20EEK
The ticket desk still sells the Soviet guidebook which boasts that the exhibits 'are really wonderful, conspicuous in their originality and can bear comparison with the best items of the world'. Exhibits from the Soviet period are now on the upper

floors, and modern ones on the ground floor, so visitors can judge the changes for themselves and whether such hyperbole applies to either era. In all fields the collections are extensive and show the Estonian dedication to pottery, weaving, glassmaking and woodwork that has surmounted all political regimes.

City Museum Vene 17; tel: 644 6553; web: www.linnamuuseum.ee [2 C3] Open Mon, Wed–Sun 10.30–18.00 Admission 30EEK

Many of the exhibits here would now be regarded as politically incorrect in the West as they concentrate on the accoutrements of the rich; life below stairs and outside the guilds and churches is ignored. Part of the museum is quite understandably called the 'Treasury', given the quantity of tapestries, silverware, pewter and porcelain displayed there. Nonetheless, the collection shows the breadth of industry and culture that developed in Tallinn from 1860 onwards. The arrival in 1870 of the railway from St Petersburg led to an increase in the population from 30,000 to 160,000 by 1917. One anniversary the Estonians were forced to celebrate in 1910 was the 200th anniversary of the Russian conquest. The museum was closed in 2000 for extensive renovations. It now shows videos of pre-war and Soviet Estonia, of the 1944 bombing, the 1980 Olympics and the 1989 demonstrations that would in due course lead to independence. Allow at least an hour to see these properly. A room of Soviet and Nazi posters has also been added. The café on the top floor is unusual in offering only homemade food. This museum is well labelled in English and the postcard sets they sell are excellent value.

Dolls' Museum Kotzebue 16; tel: 641 3491; web: www.linnamuuseum.ee Open Wed–Sun 10.30–18.00 Admission 10EEK

Opened in 1985 as a memorial to one of Lenin's closest colleagues, Mikhail Kalinin, the Dolls' Museum nonetheless even then had a small collection of toys. Kalinin is now forgotten and toys have taken over completely. The collection of dolls and dolls' houses goes back as far as the 18th century, but there are also board games, teddy bears and general toys from 1900 onwards since this is one of the few elements of Estonian life unaffected by the changing political environment. The walk from the Old Town behind the Hotel Skane [2 A3] offers a completely changed architectural environment; Tallinn on the wrong side of the tracks becomes a town of poorly maintained wooden houses and an abandoned factory. The market beside the station is worth a stop of a few minutes. Excellent light refreshments are available at prices well below those elsewhere in the town and the choice of clothes, CDs and gadgets is a good reflection of mass Estonian taste.

Energy Museum Põhja pst 29; tel: 612 4500; web: www.energiakeskus.ee [2 C1] Open Mon–Sat 10.00–17.00 Admission 30EEK

For tourists who never had the chance to visit Tirana's 'Albania Today' or Chinese museums during the Cultural Revolution, this is a splendidly flamboyant substitute. Ironically for an energy museum, many of the lights do not work but those that do illuminate graphs that all start at zero in 1945 and shoot up to the stratosphere throughout the 1950s, 1960s and 1970s. Engineers will be interested in the various meters and generators on display. The only hint of modern Estonia is an occasional photograph. The basement could not provide a greater contrast with all its striplights working and its displays of contemporary abstract art. Modern Estonia does indeed have energy but it is now portrayed more metaphorically than literally. Demonstrations of the machinery take place several afternoons a week. Check at the entrance for details.

Estonian Art Museum Kiriku plats 1; tel: 644 9340; web: www.ekm.ee [3 B5] Open Wed–Sun 11.00–18.00 Admission 20EEK
Although it looks as though it was built as an art gallery, the building housing the Estonian Art Museum was first used in the 19th century as the headquarters of the Estonian Knighthood, a major business guild. During the first independence period (1920–40) it was the Foreign Ministry and for much of the Soviet period served as the National Library. The names of the 19th- and 20th-century artists displayed here are sadly unknown outside Estonia, but many styles will be recognised by visitors. Both in the Tsarist period and under independence, most Estonian artists of note studied in Paris so the prevalent style there is reflected in their pictures. Konrad Mägi (1878–1925) is the country's most famous landscape artist and his pictures here are of many regions in Estonia. There is at present no catalogue available in English, perhaps because the collection may move to a new National Museum planned to open in the Kadriorg Park area in 2005 or 2006.

Museums

Estonian Bank Museum Estonia pst 11; tel: 668 0760; web: www.eestipank.info
[3 E6] Open Wed–Fri 12.00–17.00 Admission free
The political history of the country is mirrored in this museum through its currency.
In 1928 the kroon was tied to the British pound but it floated after 1933 when
Britain left the Gold Standard. The current building dates from 1935 and manages
to combine elements of neo-Gothic, neo-renaissance and functionalism. In its
predecessor, Estonian independence was proclaimed on February 24, 1918 and in
this one a temporary Estonian government was formed in September 1944
between the German and the Russian occupations.

Estonian History Museum Pikk 17; tel: 641 1630; web: www.earn.ee [2 C4]
Open Thu–Tue 11.00–18.00 Admission 15EEK
Dating from 1410, it was the headquarters of the Great Guild and has changed little
since. Visitors who arrive when the museum is shut can at least be consoled by the
sight of the 15th-century door knockers. Exhibits inside are well labelled in English
and concentrate on archaeology and costumes. Of more contemporary interest is
the coin collection and a section on the founding of the local freemasons in the late
1770s. They were later banned by Alexander I in 1822.

Fire-Fighting Museum Vana-Viru 14; tel: 644 4251; web: www.rescue.ee [2 E3]
Open Tue–Sat 12.00–17.00 Admission 4EEK
Like the Energy Museum, it has not changed since the Soviet era so combines the

didactic with the heroic. Dolls' houses show every possible cause of an accident in each room. Macabre photos abound of charred bodies, exploding television sets and open fires out of control. A panel lists medals awarded to local firemen until 1988 but none are listed after that year. It is a cruel comment to suggest that heroism in the Estonian fire service ceased at the restoration of independence in 1989. A number of horse-drawn and early motor fire engines are displayed. Although captions to all exhibits are only in Estonian and Russian, the staff hand out translation cards in English and German.

Health Museum Lai 28-30; tel: 641 1732; web: www.tervishoiumuuseum.ee [2 B3] Open Tue–Sat 11.00–18.00 Admission 25EEK
The Health Museum is one of the few totally contemporary museums in Tallinn and uses a range of models, toys, visual aids and colourful charts to show both adults and children the importance of healthy living. It is a brightly lit and well-thought-out display, a vivid contrast to many other museums. It may well be the only museum in the country with a hands-on element – two exercise bicycles are available for visitors. One section has been translated into Russian – that on sexually transmitted diseases.

Kalev Chocolate Museum Pikk 16; tel: 628 3811; web: www.kalev.ee [2 C3] Open Mon–Fri 10.00–15.00 Admission 10EEK
Now based at Pikk 16, above Maiasmokk Café, the Kalev Chocolate Museum originally opened in December 2000 beside the Kalev factory on the Pärnu Road to the south of

Museums

Tallinn, near the tram terminus. In 2003 the factory moved out of Tallinn and that part of the building was taken over by the police, although the amount of computer theft that accompanied this move caused them considerable embarrassment and the local population considerable amusement. Whilst the museum gives a thorough coverage of the different production techniques used in its 200-year history and visitors have the chance to smell eight different flavours, the real interest is in the political history revealed in the designs on the boxes issued during the Soviet period. In 1950, the tenth anniversary of Estonia 'joining' the USSR warranted a special box-top, even though three of those years had been spent under German occupation. Later in the 1950s, pre-war pictures of Narva were used, even though it was the Soviet army that destroyed the city in 1944. By the 1980s the authorities became aware of the knowledge Estonians now had of the West, so Mickey Mouse and Finnish television characters were allowed to join traditional Russian role models.

The history of chewing-gum in the former USSR deserves a book to itself since different politburos all devoted endless sessions to this topic. Puritans wanted it banned but the realists wanted to prove that whatever the USA could do, the USSR could do better. Production was first authorised in 1968, banned again and then reintroduced for the Olympics. Only the Kalev factory ever received the necessary authorisation.

The factory is proud that following independence in 1991 it has been able to re-establish export markets, even as far away as the United States. Perhaps a few elderly consumers there remember the Shirley Temple portrait used on boxes produced in the 1930s. Not even famous German factories are likely to be able to match the 237 varieties of marzipan produced here now. The factory shop was in a different building next door, so no hard-sell could follow a visit, but with prices about 20% lower than those charged in town or at the airport, a visit here could result in considerable savings.

Kiek in de Kök

Kiek in de Kök Komandandi 2; tel: 644 6686; web: www.linnamuuseum.ee/kiekindekok [3 C6] Open Tue–Sun 10.30–18.00 Admission 15EEK

From its initial construction in the 15th century until its completion in the late 17th century, the tower grew in height and width with walls and floors as thick as 4m, but ironically, after a Russian attack in 1577, it never saw military action again. The last time it was prepared for war was in the 1850s when the Russians feared a British invasion during the Crimean War. On the top floor, note the model of the 'plague doctor' with a waxed tunic and cape impregnated with herbs. He carries a cane with which to touch patients to avoid any risk of infection. The main exhibition on the top three floors covers Tallinn's military history. The lower floors are now used as an art gallery.

Museums

Maritime Museum Pikk 70; tel: 641 1408; web: www.tallinn.ee/meremuuseum
[2 C1] Open Wed–Sun 10.00–18.00 Admission 25EEK

Fat Margaret, the tower which holds this museum, was built between 1510 and 1529. Some walls are as much as 6m thick. In 1830 it became a prison but after being stormed in 1917 it was left as a ruin for the next 60 years. Polish restorers, famous throughout the former Soviet block, finally came to the rescue in 1978. Climb to the roof for very photogenic views of St Olav's and the town gates. The museum covers shipbuilding, cartography, port-construction and fish-breeding. There is a recent exhibit on the *Estonia* which sank off the Finnish coast on September 28 1994 with the loss of 850 lives. A model of one of the boats has political interest. It was originally named after Viktor Kingissepp, leader of the underground Estonian communist party in the early 1920s who was executed in 1924 after leading a failed attempt to overthrow the government. In 1990 it was renamed after Gustav Sule, who was Estonian javelin champion in the 1930s.

National Library Tõnismägi 2; tel: 630 7611; web: www.nlib.ee [3 C8] Open Mon–Fri 10.00–20.00 , Sat 12.00–19.00, closed Saturdays in July and August. Admission 5EEK

Day tickets for the National Library may be bought in the entrance hall, which is decorated with prints by one of Estonia's most famous contemporary artists, Eduard Wiiralt. To encourage regular use, the library has several music rooms, antiquarian and modern bookshops, a café and even piped music. On a bitter winter's day tourists may wish to await a change in the weather amongst the many English-language books and journals now available there. As one of Estonia's many preparations for entry into the EU, there are also large French, German and Scandinavian reading rooms. Normally, however, visitors should head straight for the eighth floor to view two contrasting Tallinns. To the north and east is the Tallinn of the travel posters – the spires, turrets and golden domes. In the other direction is a part of the town best seen at this distance, consisting of abandoned factories and fading tower blocks, with minimal intrusion of any colour.

Its predecessor was opened in 1918 in the parliament building on Toompea and had 2,000 books, a number that only increased to 6,000 during the 1930s. After World War II, the history of the library mirrored that of the country as a whole. Its bleakest period was until 1953 when most of the collection was of Russian books translated into Estonian. On Stalin's death the library was renamed after one of Estonia's most famous authors, Friedrich Reinhold Kreutzwald, a clear sign of a more liberal climate. By 1967 funds were specifically allocated for books in the Estonian language and in 1988, shortly before this new building was supposed to open, it was renamed the National Library and the formerly restricted sections were opened to all. The design seems to symbolise *glasnost*: light streams in through many massive windows and large open shelves display a wide cross-section of the two million books stored there. It will remain a grandiose memorial to massive public sector investment. Yet it was almost not completed. The fading Soviet government was not eager to continue funding projects outside Russia and

Museums

the new Estonian one was faced with bills it could not pay. On June 28 1989, between four and five thousand volunteers joined the building works under the slogan 'Dig a grave for Stalinism'. The director, Ivi Eenmaa, later to become mayor of Tallinn, single-handedly fought Moscow and then each new Estonian government for adequate funds and was finally able to open the library on February 22 1993, two days before National Day. Many Estonians would have liked to remove the Soviet War Memorial from the front of the museum, particularly as the sculpture is of a Red Army soldier. After much deliberation, it has been kept out of respect for the Russian-speaking population.

Natural History Museum Lai 29a; tel: 641 1738; web: www.loodusmuuseum.ee [2 B2] Open Wed–Sun 10.00–17.00 Admission 25EEK
The surprise here is that most of the exhibits are contemporary rather than historical. Whilst there is an impressive array of stuffed animals, of far greater interest is the collection of photographs of the Estonian countryside, all well lit and well labelled. The standard of English is particularly high here.

Occupation Museum Toompea 8; tel: 650 5281; web: www.okupatsioon.ee [3 C7] Open Tue–Sun 11.00–18.00 Admission 10EEK
This museum could only be opened thanks to funds provided by an Estonian-American Olga Ritso, who fled abroad in 1944 after both her father and her uncle had been killed by the Soviets. When the museum was formally opened by her and

by the Prime Minister Juhan Parts, they cut not a ribbon but barbed wire. The pathetically inadequate clothing of the prison camps is perhaps the most moving exhibit though the sight of small cases into which thousands of Estonians had to pack belongings for their Siberian exile must run a close second. The red star and a swastika are always shown side by side. To the Estonians, the Russians and the Germans are equally guilty. There are also display cases showing day-to-day life in Estonia under Soviet rule. It seems hard to believe that these items were all most Estonians knew until 1991. The cellars are now being used to display statues from Soviet times, which had all been pulled down when Estonian independence was restored in 1991. One earlier one is however missing. A statue of Stalin which had survived since 1956 could not be included; being four metres high there was no way it could be brought into the museum for display. The entrance to the museum is on Toompea, not on Pärnu.

Parliament Lossi plats 1a; tel: 631 6331; web: www.riigikogu.ee [3 B6] Open when Parliament is in session.
The façade is a simple classicist one, and all the stone and wooden materials are local. Earlier buildings on this site had usually served as a governor's residence although, in the late 19th century, the building became a prison. The earliest fort was built on this site in 1227 and the northern and western walls date from this time.
    The most famous room within the building is the White Hall, with its balcony overlooking the square. The current décor, with white cornices and a yellow ceiling,

Museums

dates from 1935. From 1922 there had been a more elaborate neo-classicist design, including ceiling mirrors and elaborate panelling. The current Parliamentary Chamber was rebuilt in 1998 and members of the public can attend debates there, but no interpretation from Estonian is provided. There are 101 members of Parliament, representing ten parties and around 20% of its members are women. Visitors are forbidden to enter 'with cold steel, firearms and pungent-smelling substances'.

Pharmacy Raekoja plats 11; tel: 631 4860 [2 C4] Open daily 10.00–18.00
Tour guides often like to point out that this business opened 70 years before Columbus discovered America. The coat of arms of the Burchart family, who ran the pharmacy for 400 years, can be seen over the entrance. Amongst the medicines they dispensed which are unlikely to find contemporary favour were fishes' eyes, lambswool and ground rubies, but patients were at least offered these potions with a glass of hot wine to help digestion. In 1725 Peter the Great summoned Burchart to St Petersburg, but he died before Burchart could reach him. In 2000 the pharmacy was extensively refurbished. Part of it is a museum and part a modern chemist's shop.

Photographic Museum Raekoja tn 4–6; tel: 644 8767; web:
www.linnamuuseum.ee [2 C4] Open Thu–Tue 10.30–18.00 Admission 10EEK
Estonia has always had a strong photographic tradition and this museum displays not only cameras produced in the country but photographs from the 19th and early 20th century. It is fortunate that many pictures from the first independence period

have survived. The basement is a gallery for the display and sale of contemporary photographs.

Theatre and Music Museum Müürivahe 12; tel: 644 6407; web: www.tallinn.ee/teatrijamuusikamuuseum [3 D5] Open Wed–Sun 10.00–17.30 Admission 15EEK

Despite its name, this museum in fact only covers music. A violin-maker's workshop has been reconstructed and the display covers most instruments of the orchestra, all of which have at some time been made in Estonia. The production of violins and pianos has a long and distinguished history in Tallinn. Very few labels are in English but, fortunately, this does not matter too much given the self-explanatory nature of the exhibits. Estonians are often accused of taking themselves too seriously; from the cartoons on the stairs, it is clear that Estonian musicians, at least, do not. No famous 20th-century conductor is spared portrayal in irreverent clothes. One violinist, Hugo Schuts, is even drawn in a bathing costume.

Town Hall Raekoja plats 1; tel: 645 7900; web: www.tallinn.ee/raekoda [2 C4] Open May 15–Sep 15 11.00–18.00 Admission 25EEK

The exterior and the interior are equally impressive. It was the administrative and judicial centre of the town and the extensive range of woodwork and paintings in the Council Chamber mainly reflect judicial themes. Six centuries of Tallinn's history have been determined in this room and, with the restoration of

Museums

independence, its role will now increase. For much of this time there were clearly ample funds in the public treasury, as is shown by the opulence of the candelabra, the money-chests and the size of the wine cellars. One of the carvings on the magistrates' bench, of David and Goliath, is often taken to symbolise the relationship between Tallinn Council and its nominal masters on Toompea in the Old Town. The Council Chamber has always been heated, unlike the neighbouring Citizens Hall. Dancing, eating and drinking at winter receptions tend to be particularly vigorous to compensate for this. The original weathervane on the top of the spire, known as Old Thomas, was destroyed in the 1944 raid but the rest of the building was spared. German architects, artists and craftsmen were employed for the Town Hall and all documents were written only in German, even during the long periods of Swedish and Russian rule. Only the tapestries have a non-German origin, being Flemish. It is sometimes possible to climb up the spire; the view from the top offers excellent shots of the Old Town for photographers but the stairs are steep so this is only recommended for the fit and determined. A large exhibition opened in the basement in summer 2003 and it is worth braving the extremely narrow staircase down to it. Plans and photographs of the square are shown as it has been, as it might have been and as it may be, together with many fragments unearthed in recent excavations. Do not forget to use the toilets here as they have been skilfully placed within the foundations.

CHURCHES

Alexander Nevsky Cathedral Tel: 644 3484 [3 B6] Open
daily 08.00–19.00

*Alexander
Nevsky
Cathedral*

The cathedral was built in 1900 on a former garden which
had housed a statue of Martin Luther. It was Alexander
Nevsky who defeated the Teutonic Knights in 1242 so the
building had a dual role in pretending to show Russian
superiority over both the Baltic Germans and the local
Estonians. It was hoped that it would help to stifle the
burgeoning nationalistic movements in Estonia, too.

Ironically, the Tsarist power that it represented was to last only a further 17 years.
Entering the cathedral represents a symbolic departure from Estonia. No-one
speaks Estonian and no books are sold in Estonian. The icons, the mosaics and the
15-ton bell were all imported from St Petersburg. Occasionally plans are discussed,
as they were in the 1930s, for the removal of the cathedral as it is so architecturally
and politically incompatible with everything else in Toompea, but it is unlikely that
any government would risk the inevitable hostility that would arise amongst the
Russian-speaking population of Tallinn.

St Charles's Church Tel: 611 9100; web: www.eelk.ee/tallinna.kaarli [3 C8]
Open daily 10.00–17.00

This massive and austere late 19th-century limestone building seats 1,500 people

Churches

and is the centre of the Estonian Orthodox Church. At a time when Russian rule was becoming more oppressive, its size discreetly symbolised Estonian nationalism. The name comes from an original wooden church built in the late 17th century during the reign of the Swedish King Charles XI. Although the church took 20 years to build, the large altar fresco was completed in ten days in 1879 by the well-known artist Johann Köler.

Dome Church Tel: 644 4140; web: www.eelk.ee/tallinna.toom [3 B5] Open daily 09.00–17.00

Work started on the Dome Church soon after the Danish invasion in the early 13th century and the first church was consecrated by King Waldemar II in 1240. It was slowly enlarged over the next four centuries as funds became available but much of the interior was destroyed in the fire of 1684 which devastated the whole of the Old Town. The Swedish King Charles XI imposed a special tax for the rebuilding of Tallinn and within two years the church had been largely restored. The baroque spire was added in 1778 so in all the church has an architectural history of over 600 years. The altarpiece, painted in 1866, is the work of the Baltic-German artist Eduard von Gebhardt. The organ, probably the most powerful in Estonia, was made in Frankfurt an der Oder in 1913 and is the last to have been imported from Germany before World War I.

The Dome Church was the religious centre for the main families of the Tallinn Baltic-German community; their coats of arms cover the church walls and their tombstones cover the floor, although a few are of Swedish origin. At the back of the church are two tombstones commemorating the butchers' and the shoemakers' guilds. The most impressive tomb, which is beside the altar, is that of the French mercenary Pontus de la Gardie who served in the Swedish army in many battles with the Russians. In the north aisle is a monument to Samuel Greig, a Scottish admiral who served in the Tsarist navy from 1763 until his death in 1788. The inscription expresses the sorrow of Catherine II at his death. Like many Scottish predecessors and successors, he had a distinguished career in this navy. He helped to destroy the Turkish fleet at the battle of Chesme in 1770 and to build up Kronstadt into a major naval base. Next to this monument is one to Adam von Krusenstern, the Baltic German who led the first Russian expedition to sail around the world, in 1803. Note the two globes, both of which omit New Zealand.

Holy Ghost Church Tel: 644 1487; web: www.eelk.ee/tallinna.puhavaimu [2 C4] Open daily 10.00–16.00

That this church does not face due east suggests that there was already a complex street layout by 1300 when building began. It was the first church to hold services in Estonian and the first extracts from the catechism in the Estonian language were printed for use here in 1535. The pulpit is the original one dating from this time. Some of the panels along the balcony, under restoration during 2003, depict Old and New Testament themes, others the life of St Elizabeth of Thuringen, the patron saint of beggars and orphans. The 1684 fire destroyed much of the interior and the

Churches

original spire but the next spire was for many years the oldest in Tallinn, dating from 1688. It was badly damaged in a fire in 2002 but was quickly replaced. Of the same age inside the church is the large wooden clock on the north wall, carved by Christian Ackermann from Königsberg. Spared from the fire was the folding altar carved in 1483 by the Lübeck artist Bernt Notke, whose *Dance Macabre* at Niguliste has already been noted. Only the organ is modern, dating from 1929; it is one of the few in Tallinn's churches built by an Estonian and not imported from Germany. To the left of the altar, the White Ensign and the plaque below it commemorate the British sailors who gave their lives between 1918 and 1920 fighting the Bolsheviks.

St Michael's Swedish Church Tel: 644 1938; web: www.eelk.ee/tallinna.rootsi [3 C5] Open daily 10.00–18.00

St Michael's does not have a tower as it was first built in the early 16th century as an almshouse and hospital. Only in the 18th century was it consecrated. The Swedish community all fled in 1944 which gave the Soviet authorities a pretext for converting the building into a sports centre, mainly used for boxing and wrestling. Generous support from the Swedish Lutheran community enabled it to be reconsecrated in 1993.

St Nicholas' Church (Niguliste) Tel: 644 9911; web: www.ekm.ee [3 C5] Open Wed–Sun 10.00–18.00

In common with many other Tallinn churches, St Nicholas' was first built in the 13th century and then expanded over the next 400 years. The original spire dated from 1696 and, being outside the town walls, the church was spared from the 1684 fire. It was, however, badly damaged during the Soviet air raid on Tallinn of March 9 1944, having had its last service the day before. The spire was firmly restored only in 1984. An earlier replacement collapsed in 1982 and the Soviet authorities flooded the streets with police to stop photographs being taken of this humiliation. (They did not completely succeed.) The carvings, chandeliers and pictures, many dating from the 16th century, had fortunately been removed before the bombing. They are all now on display again and are particularly valuable given that so much similar work in Tallinn was either destroyed in the 1684 fire or suffered from neglect in more recent times. The silver collection suffered a more precarious fate, with much being looted during World War II, but with the addition of some donations, the current exhibition is a very representative collection of Estonian work in this field from the 15th century onwards.

The interior of the church was slowly restored during the Soviet period from 1953 onwards. A small exhibition describes this work but captions in 2003 were still only in Russian and Estonian. St Nicholas' has kept its role as a museum and concert hall so has not been reconsecrated. The life of St Nicholas is portrayed in the altarpiece, over 6m wide and painted in Lübeck by Hermen Rode between 1478 and 1482. The *Dance Macabre* by Bernt Notke, another Lübeck artist, was painted a decade or so earlier and shows how nobody escapes death, whatever their powers when alive. Note the one very modern addition – a stained-glass window

Churches

by the contemporary artist, Rait Prääts, whose glass can also be seen at the National Library and the Sakala Conference Centre.

St Olav's Church Tel: 641 2241; web: www.oleviste.ee [2 C2]
Church open daily 10.00–14.00. Tower open May–Sep 11.00–17.00.
Admission 25EEK

When first built in 1267, St Olav's 140m-high steeple made it one of the tallest buildings in the world. This steeple caught fire in 1820, having been struck by lightning, and its replacement 'only' reaches 120m. It is still, however, a major feature of the Tallinn skyline and since the summer of 2002 has been open to the public. Much of the interior of the church was destroyed in the 1820 fire, as it had been in an earlier one in 1625. The rebuilding, completed in 1840, provides a contrast to most other churches in Tallinn for its plain interior. Tsar Nicholas I donated a large bell in 1850 and his generosity is noted in an inscription written, with no trace of irony, in German. The organ dates from this time but the chandeliers are earlier and have been donated from other buildings.

St Olav's Church

11

Where Tallinn is keen to show either how medieval or how modern it is, trips outside will reveal an Estonia either still trapped in the Soviet period or much more content to return to nature. Ideally, add an extra day to a Tallinn visit to allow time for some of these very different experiences.

The two islands described, Aegna and Naissaar, can be visited only in the summer, but Rocca al Mare, Kadriorg and Pirita are equally attractive under snow. The former Soviet naval base at Paldiski is macabre all year-round.

ROCCA AL MARE OPEN AIR MUSEUM

Vabaõhumuuseumi tee 12; tel: 654 9100; web: www.evm.ee

Open May–Oct daily 10.00–18.00, although the buildings close at 16.00. Open Nov–Apr daily 10.00–17.00 but the buildings are closed then. Admission 28EEK in summer and 12EEK in winter.

This museum deserves a half day to itself, ideally in balmy summer weather or after a heavy fall of snow. Take the 21 or 21b bus from the railway station and also take a sweater as protection against the wind on the many non-balmy days. A winter excursion on a sunny day is worthwhile to get some impression of what most Estonians used to endure month in, month out, every winter. Visitors at midsummer on June 23 can enjoy the all-night celebrations held here. The name in Italian means 'cliff beside the sea' and was given by the original owner of the estate when it was bought in 1863.

The museum was founded in 1957 and first opened to the public in 1964. The descriptive panels throughout are in English. It now consists of around 70 buildings

Beyond the city

and when complete should have a hundred. The aim is to show all aspects of Estonian rural architecture, with houses of both rich and poor. Most date from the 19th century but one of the chapels was built in 1699. The whole of Estonia is represented – windmills are, of course, from the island of Saaremaa but in contrast there are fishermen's cottages from Lake Peipsi on the Russian border. Even the poorest families managed to afford a sauna since to Estonians it is as crucial to living as a cooking pot. The interiors have all been appropriately furnished with kitchen utensils, weaving looms and chests of drawers.

Amongst the more unusual buildings is a tabernacle from the Herrnhut movement, a strict offshoot of the Lutheran Church. Future plans include the restoration of a Swedish cottage – about 8,000 Swedes lived in Estonia before World War II. There is already a Swedish church here, brought from the formerly Swedish-speaking village of Sutlepa. The exterior is 17th century and the interior 19th century. Inside there is a permanent exhibition of drawings from all the other Swedish churches in Estonia. In bad weather, finish your tour at the Kolu Tavern. Kolu is a village between Tallinn and Tartu, and the tavern here still has two separate bars, one originally for the gentry and one for the peasants. It serves filling, hot food such as pea soup and mashed potatoes with bacon, but do not expect any concessions to the 21st century; it remains firmly in the 19th, although a more conventional restaurant will in due course be built for more fastidious diners.

PALDISKI

Since independence, an uneasy quiet has descended on this former Soviet naval base situated 40km west of Tallinn. Unusually for Estonia, a regular train service operates from here to Tallinn, with eight services a day, the journey lasting a little over one hour. However, individual tourists would be well advised to take a car and guide for a half-day excursion as several en-route stops can be made. Estonians are more than happy to see the back of the Russian sailors but have yet to find a new role for this harbour. A daily car-ferry service to Kappelskär in Sweden started in summer 2000 which provided much-needed employment and the switching of cargo services from Tallinn soon followed, which is helping to bring a sense of hope back into the town.

Peter the Great inspected the site personally in 1715 before authorising the building of a harbour which was originally planned as the largest in the Russian Empire and for defending the country against the Swedes. It was better protected than Tallinn and ice-free for much longer. This first point was brought home to Peter very forcefully in 1717 when two boats sank in a storm whilst moored in Tallinn Harbour. From then until his death in 1825 he became obsessed with this project; the workforce was around 2,500 men supported by around 300 horses. A dam over 300m long was built. The harbour would never in fact be completed although innumerable attempts were made to do so in the 18th century. Much of the labour was supplied by prisoners; so many died of ill-treatment that Paldiski became known as the 'second Siberia'. The final straw came in 1757 when the workers' pay was reduced from two kopeks to one kopek a day and over 200 died of starvation in the months of March and April 1758 alone. The dam soon collapsed and what remained of the harbour was destroyed in a storm in 1818. Now only some of the fort remains.

In September 1939 the USSR imposed a mutual assistance pact on Estonia under which Paldiski was seized as a naval base. In May 1940, shortly before the full occupation of the country, all Estonians were expelled from the town, a practice that would be repeated all too often from 1945 in many other towns and villages along the coast. Paldiski is now the largest Soviet blot on the Estonian landscape; only the dustbins, brightly coloured and modelled on penguins with their beaks open, provide relief from piles of rubble, barbed wire and ransacked blocks of flats.

The first building to be seen on the way into the town is the former prison, but it can hardly be distinguished from much of what follows. When the Russian forces finally left in September 1995, having been granted dispensation to stay after independence, a population of around 4,000 was left with only 10% of them speaking Estonian; the remainder were Russian-speaking civilians. A curtain behind a window, an occasional light or even the sight of an occasional human being, shows that life has not totally died out here but the slogan in the town's English-language brochure, *A Town with a Future*, seemed at the time to be a joke in particularly bad taste. However, in 2000 a new hotel was opened, the **White Ship** (Valge Laev) at Rae 32 (tel: 674 2095; web: www.weekends.ee). 'Welcome aboard' mats are behind each entrance, a porthole is on the door of every room and maritime memorabilia cover all the walls. It would be possible to commute into Tallinn from here, and when Tallinn hotels are full, late bookers will have no choice.

Returning to Tallinn, two very contrasting stops can be made. Shortly after independence, a monument was erected in the forest at Klooga to commemorate the massacre of 2,000 Jews there on September 19 1944, just before the German withdrawal. The small Estonian-Jewish community had already been killed by then; these victims were largely from other eastern European countries. The former village of Tabasalu is now the first of Tallinn's suburbs, most of whose inhabitants have much more money than sense or taste. The money stands out, but it is well protected by high walls and rottweilers. A few poultry farmers remain on the outskirts of the village but it cannot be long before they are bought out.

AROUND TALLINN BAY

Allow a full day to visit the island of Aegna, the yacht harbour at Pirita and the park at Kadriorg. Several buses serve Pirita from the town centre and the journey takes about ten minutes. The relevant bus stop is one beyond that for the hotel.

Aegna

Boats to and from Aegna operate out of Pirita harbour from a small jetty beside the café, not from the larger jetty beside the hotel and yacht club. Boats leave for the island around 09.00, at 12.00 and in the early evening. Check timings at the tourist office or via a hotel reception before setting off and do not forget an umbrella in case the weather suddenly changes. Tickets cost 80EEK (£3.50/US$5.50) for the round trip.

Aegna is so quiet that even Estonians are prepared to turn off their mobile phones, and neither the Germans nor the Russians were able to leave their mark. Conifer trees abound, as do minute beaches, and the few open areas have been made available for camping. Much of the island can be seen in the three hours allowed by the morning boat schedule though a full day of peace and quiet is what most local visitors seek. Paths are clearly marked and a detailed map is displayed at the harbour.

Pirita, Viimsi and Kadriorg Palace

Pirita was built as the Olympic village for the yachting and sailing events of the 1980 Olympics. For a precious three weeks Tallinn briefly returned to being an international city. An array of consumer goods, Western newspapers and direct international telephone dialling suddenly came to Tallinn and left equally suddenly when the games were over. Only the buildings have remained and they are so obviously of Soviet design that the harbour hardly seems to belong to modern Estonia. On returning to Pirita, visitors of Estonian origin may wish to take the 34 bus for 2km inland to **Metsakalmistu**, the Forest Cemetery. Most famous Estonians are buried in this pine forest, including the writer A H Tammsaare, the poetess Lydia Koidula and the chess player Paul Keres. Since independence, the body of Konstantin Päts, president until the Soviet occupation, has been returned and he is now buried here together with his immediate family. He died in a Soviet psychiatric hospital in 1956. The body of General Laidoner, however, still lies in 2001 in a communal grave in Vladimir Prison where he died in March 1953, despite strong pressure from the Estonian government for it to be formally identified and returned. His wife was released from prison in 1954 after his death but was only allowed to return to Estonia after her 70th birthday. She had been a pianist and took some music with her to Siberia, practising on walls and tables to keep her fingers fit. Johan Laidoner was commander-in-chief for much of the pre-war period and his former house on the Viimsi Peninsula, about 5km from Pirita, is now the **Laidoner Museum**.

The most moving exhibit is a French–Russian dictionary given to him during his imprisonment in 1944; he used several pages of it to compose his political testament. It ends, in English, with the words 'Estonia, with all thy faults, I love thee still. Johan Laidoner'. Considering how jealous Stalin was of his reputation, it is remarkable how many items associated with him and with this house have survived. During Soviet times the KGB had taken it over in order to break completely the links with Estonian independence.

The museum was greatly expanded in 2001 and again in 2003. With the help of the Imperial War Museum in London there is now a British Room, covering the navy's role in helping to establish Estonian independence in 1918–20. It is expected that many more exhibits will soon come from Britain. This would be appropriate in view of Laidoner's often quoted remark, 'Without the arrival of the British fleet in Tallinn in December 1918, Estonia and the other Baltic states would have found themselves in the hands of the Bolsheviks.' The Poles have likewise opened a room in honour of Marshal Pilsudski who played a similar role to Laidoner in ensuring his country's independence from Russia.

Other visitors will head for the main harbour and the entrance to the **Lembit** submarine beside the petrol station. No brochures are available but the sailors on board speak reasonable English and their enthusiasm on meeting the few English-speaking visitors who bother to come more than compensates for any linguistic failings. Two submarines were originally commissioned from Barrow-in-Furness by the Estonian navy in 1936. *Kalev*, the second one, was sunk in October 1941, by which time both had been taken over by the Soviet navy and taken from Tallinn before it fell to the Germans. The *Lembit* saw service throughout World War II, being used mainly to attack German cargo ships en route to Sweden. Its torpedoes had a range of 12km and it could sink below the surface for up to 24 hours. Its speed reached 60km/h. It remained in service until 1955, after which it was used for training. The Soviets made no attempt to conceal the British origin of the submarine, so many of the original features remain. The *Lembit* was closed for restoration in 2003 and may not be ready to reopen in 2004.

The walk back to the centre of Tallinn is two or three miles. Cross the main road from the harbour to the site of **St Birgitta's Convent**. Although the convent is included in most sightseeing tours, walking here can be a precarious experience as the ruins are so badly maintained. The convent lasted intact for only 170 years, from

1407 until the siege of 1577 when it was largely destroyed by troops of Ivan IV in the Livonian Wars. The outline of the main body of the church is clear; the western gable together with the vestry, cloister and refectories can be identified. Minor restoration and excavation work started in 1960 and was brought to a close only in 2001. The new convent on the north side was completed in 2000 and part of the building is used as a hotel (see page 56).

Staying on the land-side of the main road, after half a mile is the **Soviet War Memorial**. It could hardly be anything else, given its size and the military themes of the bronze statues. The Estonians carry out minimal maintenance here but, as with all Soviet war memorials, they are not removed and Russians congregate on the days of the old Soviet holidays such as May Day and November 7. The text is particularly offensive to Estonians as the monument is dedicated to 'Fighters for Soviet Power'. It was completed only in 1975. A Soviet guidebook excuses this long delay by claiming 'at last Estonian artists had enough skill and adequate economic means to complete such an ensemble'.

St Birgitta's Convent

Around Tallinn Bay

The obelisk dates from 1960 and commemorates the hurried departure from Tallinn of the Bolshevik fleet in 1918 when German forces occupied the town.

An even more dominant landmark from the Soviet era is the **TV Tower**, about a mile inland from Pirita on Kloostrimetsa. Going there by bus, expect to be surrounded by elderly Russians with flowers since the Russian cemetery and crematorium are nearby. The few tourists who now visit the tower also seem to be Russian. This is a pity as it does provide an extensive view of the town and port not available elsewhere. The entrance is as flamboyant as one would expect; the windows are of stained glass, with portraits of valiant industrial workers; covered aisles surround basins of fountains which in turn are surrounded by lawns. However, nothing has been maintained properly (except for the lifts inside) so moss and weeds become ever more prominent. Nobody has bothered to put Estonian signs in the lift or change the menu in the revolving tower restaurant from smoked fish and chicken Kiev. The telescope still takes kopek coins.

A few hundred yards further along this road is **Maarjamäe Palace** [1 E1], which has probably had one of the most turbulent ownership histories of any site in Tallinn. Maarjamäe means 'Mary's Hill' but the German name, Streitberg ('Hill of Strife'), was for many centuries more appropriate. The only consolation is that the blood shed here spared Tallinn itself from many battles. The final one took place in the early 18th century as Russia seized the Baltics from the Swedes during the Northern Wars. To set the seal on his conquest, Peter the Great established Kadriorg Park as a summer residence, so many of the St Petersburg nobility felt obliged to followed suit. Those who could not immediately afford the luxury of a suitable building subsidised it with a factory, so lime kilns and sugar refineries adjoined the manor houses. The sugar was sold in Riga and St Petersburg and the plant was run on British coal. A fire in 1868 destroyed much of the factory and it was never rebuilt. In the 1870s, when the estate was bought by Count Anatoli Orlov-Davydov from St Petersburg, the rebuilding he ordered came to deserve the title 'palace'. Terraces, a gateway decorated with copper eagles and the Gothic tower gave it an almost regal air. The Dutch Consulate bought it in the 1920s when the Orlov-Davydovs emigrated to France and continued its use as a summer residence. It was to lose its appeal in this role when in 1926 the road to Pirita was built across the grounds, cutting off the manor house from direct and private access to the sea. However, the road brought with it commercial potential which was eventually realised in a hotel and restaurant called the Riviera Palace. In 1937 the Estonian air force took it over as a training school and they are sadly responsible for the dreary façade at the front of the building. From 1940 until 1975, when Maarjamäe became a museum, the Soviet military used but did not abuse it. During the 1980s, Polish restorers finally brought the building back to its turn-of-the-century glory, turning their attention to the chandeliers, fireplaces, parquet floors and ceilings. It is ironic that one of the last Soviet legacies to Tallinn should be the perfect surroundings for a museum which chronicles Estonian independence.

Although few labels are in English and the one available guidebook is now badly out of date, this is without doubt the best museum in Tallinn. New rooms are constantly being added, exhibits are generously displayed, the layout is sensibly planned and there is the complete absence of benign neglect that seems to permeate so many other Tallinn museums. It covers Estonian history from the mid 19th century until the present day. It amply contrasts the lifestyles of rich and poor and shows the diversity of industrial products and international contacts that the country enjoyed during the first period of independence between the two world wars. It even had a thriving tourist board whose brochures displayed here sold Estonia as 'The Cheapest and Most Interesting Country in Europe'. One room opened in the summer of 1998 is devoted to the life of Konstantin Päts, Estonia's president between the two world wars. On more contemporary themes, the anti-Soviet guerrilla movement and the return to independence are covered movingly but not bombastically. Amongst new themes covered in rooms opened in 2000 are the battle for Tallinn in early 1918 and the German occupation from 1941–44.

Behind the palace is one of the few late-1950s' constructions of which Estonians can be fiercely proud – the **Song Festival Amphitheatre** [1 E1]. It has the massive grandeur to be expected from that time but is not wasteful of materials and does not dominate the surrounding area. The parabola provides cover for 5,000 singers and up to 20,000 more have often taken part. The most famous recent festival took place in 1989, when the previously banned national anthem, *My Native Land*, was sung by an audience of around 300,000 people, 20% of the entire population of the country. In winter, the steep slope at the back of the parabola provides Tallinn's only ski- and toboggan-run. Note the plaques at the top of the slope which commemorate each of the Song Festivals held every five years since 1869. The tower was opened to the public in 2000 and gives photographers good shots of the Old Town and the port combined.

Returning to the shoreline, at the junction of the roads to Pirita and to Narva, note the **Russalka (Mermaid) Memorial** [1 D2], which commemorates the sinking of a battleship with this name in 1893. It depicts an angel looking out to sea. Do not be surprised to see Russian-speaking wedding couples laying flowers here on a Saturday. The sculptor, Amandus Adamson, is one of Estonia's most famous, and perhaps because of this monument he was granted official respect in the Soviet period and a memorial bronze bust of him stands in Kadriorg Park. The park is the next stage of the walk and one corner is just behind the Russalka Memorial. The park, and **Kadriorg Palace** [1 D2] which forms its centrepiece, was built immediately following Peter the Great's first visit to Tallinn in 1718 with his Italian architect Niccolo Michetti. The triumphal decoration of the ceiling in the Great Hall celebrates his defeat of the Swedes in the Northern War and is loosely based on Rembrandt's *Diana and Actaeon*. The hunter being torn apart by his dogs can be seen to symbolise the Swedish King Charles XII being let down by his army. Sadly the building was not completed by 1725 when Peter the Great died and no subsequent Tsar ever showed the commitment that he did. In fact Catherine I never came to Tallinn again after his death. Perhaps the description often given of the palace as a 'mini-Versailles' is fair, as what was carried out does show some French and Italian influence. A fire destroyed much of the interior in 1750 and it was subsequently never again used by the Russian royal family. In 1930 Kadriorg Palace became the official residence of the Estonian president but now houses the Foreign Art Museum, the collection being mainly Flemish and Baltic-German.

None of the furniture was originally here. The Russian royal family took furniture with them as they travelled between their palaces and also 'borrowed' extensively from the local nobility. Much of this collection is what the Baltic Germans had to leave in their manor houses when Hitler 'called them home' in October 1939. Despite the cool personal and state relations with the Russians, a lot of furniture was still ordered from St Petersburg during the first independence period (1920–40). However, the room devoted to Soviet art from the 1920s is likely to be of most interest to visitors. The designs on the porcelain show the most immediate break with the past as all the themes are 100% political. It would take another ten years before painting was similarly controlled. Some of this porcelain was prepared for the first Soviet Art Exhibition held in St Petersburg in 1923, by which time the St Petersburg Imperial Porcelain Factory had become the State Porcelain Factory. It came to be known as 'agitation porcelain'. Many rooms have been restored to their original 1930s' layout, when President Päts lived here. The Danzig-baroque library is the most elaborate room and was completed only in 1939, a year before the Soviet take-over. The salon has a wooden drinks cabinet with panels portraying scenes from *Kalevipoeg*, the 19th-century Estonian national epic. The palace reopened in 2000 and then work started on re-landscaping the surrounding gardens. This should be completed by 2004.

Kadriorg Park [1 D2] is a year-round joy for local people and tourists alike. In winter the combination of sun and snow amidst the trees and sculptures offers a peaceful contrast to the hectic commercial life of Tallinn just a few hundred metres away. Spring brings out the blossom of the cherry and ash trees, summer the swans, the squirrels and the fountains and autumn the blends of gold and red as the trees shed their leaves. A cottage in the park used by Peter the Great during the construction of the palace now poses as a museum but the paucity of exhibits perhaps redefines the word 'minimalist'. A bare main room, a few photographs and some haphazard items of furniture would be best concealed from tourists entitled to expect much more.

A hundred metres back towards town, on Weizenbergi opposite the main entrance to Kadriorg Palace, the **Mikkeli Museum** [1 D2] will quickly restore the enthusiasm of a visitor. This building was the palace kitchen but in 1997 was opened to house the collection of Estonia's most fortunate private art collector, Johannes Mikkel. Born in 1907 (and in 2003 still alive), he was able to start buying during the first independence period when departing Baltic Germans and Russian nobles abandoned enormous quantities of paintings, porcelain and prints. He was allowed to trade during the Soviet period and enhanced his collection with items bought in the Caucasus and Central Asia. There is no predominant theme, but the quality and taste of every item stands out, be it a piece of Kangxi or Meissen porcelain, a Dürer woodcut, a Rembrandt etching or any one of his 20 Flemish paintings. Folders in English are available in every room with descriptions of all major exhibits and modern lighting ensures that each item is viewed as well as possible.

On leaving the museum and turning left, a slight detour can first be made to the far side of the lake behind the Mikkeli building. The splendidly isolated house at Roheline 3 is the **Eduard Vilde House Museum** where Estonia's most prolific writer, both at home and in exile all over Europe, spent the final six years of his life between 1927 and 1933. Typically for most established Estonians at that time, the furnishings are simple and there are many empty spaces. Return to Weizenbergi to continue back into town. At the corner of Poska on the left, house number 20a has some baroque imitation of the palace although it was built only in 1939. A good place to rest is the Café Omabi on the other corner. Apart from one microwave, modern Estonia has passed it by almost entirely: the food is freshly prepared for each order, there is no menu in English and no piped music. Beside it is Käsitoo, a souvenir shop sensibly patronised by overseas Estonians as its prices are not geared to cruise passengers or Finnish day-trippers. Weizenbergi lasts a further 300m or so before joining Narva mnt. Every house is probably now owned, or was before World War II, by a famous Estonian. Ladas or small Toyotas may be parked in the street, but considerable wealth is discreetly hidden behind the lace curtains. The turn-of-the-century, four-storey houses display hints of Jugendstil, whilst the wooden ones are characteristic of middle-class suburbs throughout Estonia. On a neighbouring street, Koidula, one of the largest wooden houses belonged to Estonia's most famous author, A H Tammsaare, who died in March 1940. In his honour it is now the Tammsaare Museum but labelling is only in Estonian and

Russian. The only English translations of his work were published in Moscow in the 1970s and are now out of print. The exhibition has hardly been changed since the Soviet era so it presents him as far more of a 'man of the people' than was really the case. Tammsaare is depicted on the 25EEK note and it is perhaps significant that it is his farm that is pictured on the reverse, not this townhouse. Some downstairs rooms are now used for modern art exhibitions, which provide a much-needed splash of colour in contrast to the gloom upstairs.

At the junction of Weizenbergi and Narva mnt there is a taxi rank and bus stop. A large Methodist church has recently been built on the far side; otherwise Narva mnt from here back to the Viru Gate is totally devoted to mammon. There is no point in describing any of the buildings since they are mainly being pulled down to give way to glass skyscrapers. This area will soon be Tallinn's Wall Street or Square Mile. A Japanese restaurant has already opened to ensure a serious and affluent gastronomic ambience.

NAISSAAR

If Tallinn is cutting-edge, dynamic and every other cliché associated with the capitals of the EU accession countries, the island of Naissaar is the complete opposite. Its website remains only in Estonian and its boat schedules a state secret until the service starts sometime in early summer. Sometimes a day trip is possible; sometimes schedules require an overnight stay in one of the cottages adapted into hostels. The boat goes from the same jetty just beyond Pirita that is used by the

Aegna boat. The electricity supply, usually limited to two hours in the morning and two in the evening, imposes a firm schedule for going to bed and for getting up. Visitors are not allowed to bring alcohol with them but there is one café that can supply the modest needs in this field of most visitors. Yet those who take a four-hour walking tour will be amply rewarded by seeing the legacies not only of those who lived there but also of those who succeeded in occupying the island, as well as those who, like the British Royal Navy, just dropped by for a few months. It is advisable to pre-book a guide, if only to be sure of avoiding areas where there could still be unexploded mines, the worst of several Soviet legacies.

Naissaar has had to reinvent itself several times during the 250 years since it began to be regularly inhabited. The name means 'women's island' but there is no clear origin for this name, only fanciful and largely unprintable legends. Ironically, it has in fact been male-dominated for most of its occupation with women having far less importance than on the mainland. The early Swedish-speaking settlers who came in the mid-18th century were fishermen who traded their catches and spruce in Tallinn for the agricultural goods that the sandy windswept terrain on the island did not allow them to grow. Many in fact had lived in Finland and they came to escape the Tsarist seizure of Finland from the Swedes. Naissaar was free from plague then and also free from Baltic-German landlords, which encouraged a community of around 200–300 to settle there; the population stayed around this level until World War II. A Swedish primary school was established in 1874 and an Estonian one in 1925. In winter, the island was always cut off for several weeks at a time when the ice was too thick for the boats to secure a passage, but too thin for horses or, later, cars to cross. The few affluent islanders were invariably pilots who guided foreign trading ships into Tallinn harbour. Captains unwilling to pay their fees could find their boats shipwrecked around Naissaar and the cargoes that were salvaged provided a useful addition to income from fishing. In 1854, the British navy occupied the island for a few months as part of its attempt to blockade supplies from reaching Russia during the Crimean War. This was long enough for them to show the islanders how to play cricket, but the game did not catch on.

The population was first deported by the Russians in 1730 when they built a fortress to defend the island from possible Swedish attacks. There would be three further deportations by the Russians in the 20th century. The first occasion was in 1914 as the Tsarist armies tried to defend it from the Germans. The second was in 1940 at the start of the first Soviet occupation. Residents were assured that they would not have to pay for transport to the mainland and were invited to pass on any special wishes to the authorities. The third deportation was in 1944 when the Soviets returned after the Germans had retreated to Latvia. It would be 50 years before any Estonian could live there again.

Visitors are likely to stay in the village of **Männiku**, about 2km from the port, where the island administrative centre and café is based. The houses look reasonably modern but very un-Soviet with the use of light woods and extensive glass. This is because they were all prefabricated in Finland and were part of the reparations demanded by the Soviet Union from Finland at the end of World War

II. The larger Soviet buildings, including the factory that produced the mines, have all been abandoned but a schoolroom has been converted into an amusing museum. Much has been left as the Russians abandoned it, with posters proclaiming *perestroika*, unread books by Lenin and enormous radiograms. Two waxworks have been added of Soviet marines, one asleep and one on the toilet. The narrow-gauge railway ends here and can sometimes be taken for a ride back to the port.

The now abandoned village of **Lõunaküla** is on the southern shore of the island and until World War II was its centre. Not a single house now remains from that time. The shell of the church is from one built in 1934 by the Swedish Lutheran Church. It replaced an earlier one built in 1856 but burnt down by the Bolsheviks during their brief occupation of the island in 1918. The **cemetery** built beside the shore contains the graves of sailors who died not in battle on the island but at sea. It was not built beside the church since the catholic French soldiers could not be buried on Lutheran ground.

LAHEMAA NATIONAL PARK

Situated along the north coast of Estonia, about 100km from Tallinn en route to Narva, Lahemaa National Park and the buildings within it show both the Baltic-German and the Soviet occupation at their most benevolent. The von der Pahlen family, which owned Palmse Mansion, the architectural high point of a visit to the park, contributed to Estonia for two centuries with their administrative, commercial and academic activities. Whilst to the west, the Soviets would blight the outskirts of Tallinn with shoddy tower blocks and to the east ransack the coast with oil-shale exploitation, Lahemaa, the Land of Bays, was given the status of a protected national park in 1971 and great efforts were made to support and enhance the wildlife of the area. Similar support was given to restoration of the manor houses and fishing villages. The boundaries of the park stretch for 40km along the coast and include several islands. Most Estonians, and all foreigners, were forbidden to enter the park because of its proximity to the coast but this did at least prevent any tourist and industrial development. Building work is now restricted to the minimum necessary to grant access to visitors and to provide for their stay.

Getting there

Within a full day, it is possible to cover most sights and return to Tallinn the same day. Given the distances between major sites, hiring a car or joining a group tour is the best way to travel around the park. Group tours are arranged by local tour operators (see page 39). Taking a taxi is also surprisingly reasonable.

A bus service operates twice daily from Tallinn to Palmse and Sagadi, and more frequently to Võsu and Viitna. There is also a twice-daily bus service from Haljala into the park. Many of the buses going east from Tallinn to Narva stop at Viitna and Haljala. A limited bus service operates within the park, but stops are always conveniently situated close to the manor houses or in the village centres. Cyclists can bring their bikes on the many public buses that link the villages of Võsu, Käsmu and Palmse with Tallinn and Rakvere.

Lahemaa National Park

Touring the park

Leave the St Petersburg Highway from Tallinn to Narva at Viitna and then drive through Palmse, Sagadi, Altja, Võsu, Käsmu, Viinistu and Kolga before returning to the main road 18km further west. Drivers starting from the east or south will come off the main road at Haljala and begin the tour at Sagadi. Viitna is best known for its coaching inn, which dates from 1791. Like so many buildings in Estonia, it was destroyed at some stage in its history by fire; what is surprising is that the fire here was in 1989. Let us hope that it is the last serious fire to blight Estonian architecture. The inn appeals most in mid-winter with its open fire and substantial portions of food, but at all times of year offers a good respite from the dull drive between Tallinn and the Russian border at Narva. It is no longer a hotel, but in the days of horse-drawn transport it served this function, being a day's ride from Tallinn. The inn was clearly divided into two sections so that masters and servants would not eat together.

Palmse Manor

The manor is 6km off the main road, the perfect distance to ensure easy access but equally to ensure a totally calm natural environment. It is without doubt the most impressive manor house in Estonia and the 15 years of restoration between 1971 and 1986 have left a lasting and appropriate memorial to the von der Pahlen family. The main building and the surrounding gardens were begun in 1697 but the Northern War between Sweden and Russia halted construction. It was completed in 1740 and then work started on the other buildings. The family lived here until 1923, when the estate was nationalised in accordance with the Land Law of 1919. The land was then divided amongst ten families and the house became a convalescent home; after World War II the Soviet administration converted it into a pioneer camp for young people. The other buildings had all

Palmse Manor

been left to decline and by 1972, when restoration began, were in such poor condition that it was necessary to consult drawings and photographs from the turn of the century to see their original format. Different histories like to typecast both the architecture of the manor house and the landscaping of the gardens. The former has been labelled French, Dutch and Italian, the latter English and Chinese. None of these are helpful as the von der Pahlens wanted a tasteful, solid and modest environment both indoors and outdoors and used largely local materials. They had no desire or need for ostentation as they all had highly successful careers in many different fields. They distilled as profitably as they ran the Baltic Railway Company; their paintings are as worthy as their botanical research. Apart from one episode in 1805, their 200-year rule passed without peasant unrest and the famous Estonian writer of the 19th century, Friederich

Reinhold Kreutzwald, puts this down to the relationship between the family and their farmers being similar to that between parents and children. They shunned military activity and the only sign of Prussian patriotism is the name they gave in 1871 to one of the paths through the wood – Parisian Way – following the defeat of the French by the Prussian Army the previous year.

Apart from one chair in the main bedroom, and the chandelier in the reception, none of the furniture is original but the items that have been collected from all over Estonia are similar to those the family would have used. The chairs in the concert hall have all been recently produced, but follow the original designs. The late 19th-century music box is still in working order and plays 24 different pieces, mainly dance music. The drawings and charts on the first floor are by the 20th-century artist Olev Soans (1925–95) although many are modelled on 19th-century originals. On the balustrade are two monograms, one from the von der Pahlen family in 1785 and one added two hundred years later to commemorate the restoration in 1985. The tiled stoves throughout the house are original, as are the two granite obelisks that guard the entrance. To the left of the main building is a small wooden one which looks like a small chapel. It has the German name 'Kavalierhaus', which defies translation into English but was where the younger people congregated. Now it would be a computer centre by day and a disco by night but, in the early 19th century, sedate dancing could take place for much of the day. Its current use is as a discreet souvenir shop. To the right of the main building is the former bath house, which has now been converted into a café.

Further left is the orchard and the greenhouse, testimony to several generations of botanists in the family. Sadly the greenhouse no longer cultivates the plums, apricots and pineapples which used to enhance the family meals. The distillery has been converted into a hotel and although it serves a wide range of Estonian spirits, none are now produced within the confines of the park. The former stables are now an information centre for the whole park and the shop there sells a wider range of maps and guides than does the souvenir shop. Particularly useful in this respect are two leaflets, Viru Bog Nature Trail and Lahemaa Birds. A walk along the lakeside is worthwhile, if only for the view back to the main house, but it can then be extended by taking one of the many different trails through the woods. Of sociological rather than architectural interest is the monument to the von der Pahlens erected in 1933 by the ten families who took over their land which shows the affection with which they were still regarded a decade after their departure. More impressive, although untouched by humans, are the erratic boulders, the massive lumps of granite that cluster in several places in the woods.

Sagadi

Sagadi is a 6km drive from Palmse and its manor house is very different. Local writers prefer it to Palmse, making comparisons with the chateaux on the Loire and even with the Garden of Eden. Travellers arriving with such expectations will definitely be disappointed, but those with a more open mind will see how a typical Baltic-German family lived and ruled. The land was owned by the von Fock family from the 17th century, but the current building, and those immediately surrounding it, date largely from the 1750s. Construction was not therefore hindered by the Northern War, which halted work at Palmse. The façade was rebuilt in 1795, with the addition of the balcony. The von Focks had a variety of business careers, largely in shipbuilding and in forestry, but none reached the eminence of the von der Pahlens. The family lived in the building until 1939 although, following the Land Law of 1919, the estates were nationalised and the main building became a primary school. It kept this function until 1970, and soon afterwards full restoration of the whole estate began. Some of the furniture is original but, as at Palmse, many pieces have been brought from other houses that were not restored. The carpet in the banqueting hall is from Aubusson in France and belonged to President Konstantin Päts. It is worth making the tortuous ascent to the first floor to see the collection of stuffed animals. The Forestry Museum used to be in the main house, but has recently been extended and is now in an annexe. Some labels are in English. The craft shops in the former stables offer a wide selection of souvenirs at prices much lower than those charged by shops in Tallinn.

Altja

The fishing village of Altja is 8km from Sagadi. It has never been much more than a hamlet but it suffered under the Soviet regime when fishing, its sole livelihood, was banned and the population dropped from around 120 down to merely 20. Subsistence farming was hardly a substitute as only potatoes could grow in the sandy soil and the grazing lands supported only a minimal number of cattle or oxen. Fishing is now being revived and the excellent inn, which tourist groups use, provides employment during the summer. Although outsiders, even Estonians, were not allowed access to the coast at that time, restoration of the wooden buildings started in 1971. The inn dates from the early 19th century and, for most its life, women were not admitted except on March 25, Lady Day. Most of the buildings are not in fact inhabited but are netsheds for storing boats and fishing equipment. There are several walks along the coast, and paths have been cleared between the erratic boulders. Given the isolation and, in the winter, the desolation of this village, it is hard to picture it a hundred years ago as an affluent port where the fishermen and boat builders could enjoy coffee and wine.

Võsu

Eighteen kilometres to the west lies the seaside resort of Võsu, popular throughout the summer with Estonian families. It was quite a grand resort in the 19th century but has since broadened its appeal, families in the 1920s coming here by ferry from Tallinn. Yet it is never overcrowded and the pine woods that back on to the beach make for pleasant short walks both in the summer and on a bright winter's day in the snow. For a grotesque Soviet experience the restaurant opposite the Merehotell can be 'recommended'. It does not merit a name so is simply called Soogisaal ('eating hall'). For bleak décor, surly staff, lack of hygiene and poor food, it has no equal anywhere in Estonia.

Lahemaa National Park

Käsmu

The village of Käsmu is a further 8km along the coast. When built in the early 19th century, it was often known as 'millionaire's village', such were the profits made from salt smuggling. In the 1920s smuggling shifted to alcohol when Finland attempted to impose prohibition. Finland gave up this aim in April 1932 and Käsmu suffered considerably. A macabre end to this traditional role came in June 1940 when many likely victims of Soviet hostility were smuggled out of Estonia before the whole country was occupied.

Käsmu is clearly no ordinary fishing village and this early prosperity shows signs of returning as affluent Tallinn businessmen buy up the former captains' houses. The main building is the Maritime Museum which previously served as a navigation college during the first period of independence and then as a coastguard station in the Soviet period. The large watchtower beside the building of course dates from the latter, when swimming was banned after 21.00, such was the supposed risk that escapes to Finland might be made under the cover of darkness. The museum has two unique features in that there is no admission charge and it is open at any time. The owner, Aarne Vaik, spent 20 years collecting material surreptitiously for the museum when there was no chance of displaying it. At present the collection concentrates on the 1920s and 1930s but it will eventually be extended through World War II and the Soviet period. A natural history section to cover sea fauna and flora is also being planned. One item of particular interest to British tourists is the £1 note from 1919; with all local currencies at that time being so insecure, sterling was the only acceptable currency for maritime insurance.

Beside the village church is the Baron Dellingshausen Memorial, perhaps unique in being built by him to feign his death. He was implicated in the failed plot to kill Tsar Alexander II in 1881 and fled to Germany with this memorial as a safeguard against the police looking for him. The false tomb was soon discovered but the Baron was able to die of natural causes in the safe environment of Potsdam. The building now houses a photographic exhibition of local people at work and at home, all the pictures having been taken in 1999.

Viinistu

Visitors who turned up in this village during the 1990s would have found a village that modern Estonia had completely ignored. Thanks though to a former manager of Abba, the continuingly successful Swedish pop group, it has suddenly become mainstream.

Jaan Manitski, who was born here in 1943, could chart his family links to the area stretching back 400 years, so when the family fled to Sweden in 1944, they always hoped to return. He did so in 1989 when, having made a fortune, he decided that money was no longer of great importance to him. He compared it to cow dung: something useful in small doses but which stinks in larger quantities. His first work in Viinistu was growing mushrooms; he then had a short spell as Estonian foreign minister where he caused havoc in the accounts department when he left by not bothering to claim his last month's salary. He is now part-owner of Estonia's major daily paper *Eesti Päevaleht* but what he will definitely be remembered for is the Viinistu Art Museum, which opened in 2003.

As Estonian museums are obliged to have an admission fee, and Manitski could not prevent this even in a private collection, he provides coffee and biscuits for the 10EEK he is forced to charge. Visitors are rewarded with the best collection of 20th-century Estonian art in the whole country, and in particular with works by Konrad Mägi (1878–1925) and Eduard Viiralt (1898–1954). The collection is being extended and several rooms are devoted to temporary exhibitions, some of which will undoubtedly shock more sensitive visitors, who may prefer to limit their viewing to the permanent collection. The building is beside the sea and a hotel nearby is due to be opened in 2005. Rich Estonians who patronise the arts are very rare; as more business people enjoy the success that Jaan Manitski did, let us hope they follow in his footsteps.

Kolga

Kolga is 30km west of Käsmu so can be visited on the way back to Tallinn. The estate was originally a monastery, but in 1581 the Swedish King gave it to his French army commander Pontus de la Gardie as a reward for his military prowess. He himself hardly used it as he was drowned in the Narva River four years later in 1585, but the property stayed in his family until the mid 17th century when Christina de la Gardie married the Swedish Admiral Otto Stenbock. The 'Stenbock era' was to last until 1940 when the family returned to Sweden at the time of the Soviet occupation. Sadly the estate was then allowed to degenerate and only in 1980 did maintenance and restoration begin. Much remains to be done but a visit is still worthwhile as it is easy to picture how impressive the whole area must have been. The classical columns surmounted by the Stenbock coat of arms were built at the turn of the 18th and 19th centuries when the family was at its most prosperous, thanks to its successful distilling and farming. It is to be hoped that such prosperity quickly returns to the area.

12

PRONUNCIATION
Words in Estonian are pronounced with the stress on the first syllable. Individual letters are pronounced as follows:

Vowels
a as the English **u** in **but**
aa is like **a** in **father**
e as in **bet**
ee as in the English **eh** or French **de**
i as in **pin**
ii as **ee** in **feel**
o as in **off**
oo as **eau** in the French **peau**
u as in **put**
uu as the **oo** in **food**
ä almost as in **cat**, but with a less open mouth
ää is the same as **ä**, but with more open mouth
ö as **ir** in **girl**, but with rounded lips
öö as the **oeu** in the French **voeu**
õ is peculiar to Estonian and is pronounced with the lips in the position of a short **e** while the tongue is retracted
õõ is the same as **õ**, but longer

ü is produced by pronouncing **i** with a protrusion of the lips and a narrow opening of the mouth

üü is the same as ü, but longer and clearer

Consonants

b is voiceless, almost like the **p** in **copy**

d is voiceless as the **t** in **city**

g is voiceless as the **ck** in **ticket**

k, **p** and **t** are stronger and longer than the voiceless **g**, **b**, and **d**

h is the same as in English, but less aspirated

j like **y** in **you**

l as in **lily**

m is the same as in English, but shorter

n as in English

r is trilled

s is voiceless and weaker than the English **s**

v as in English

z as the **s** in **was**

USEFUL WORDS AND EXPRESSIONS
Greetings and basic communication

hello	*tere*
goodbye	*nägemist*
good morning	*tere hommikust*
good evening	*head õhtust*
goodnight	*head ööd*
yes	*jah*
no	*ei*
please	*palun*
thank you	*tänan*
less	*vähem*
a little (more)	*(natuke) rohkem*
enough	*küllalt*
now (later)	*praegu (hiljem)*
How long?	*Kui kaua?*
How much (is it)?	*Kui palju (see maksab)?*
When?	*Millal?*
Where (is)?	*Kus (on)?*
Excuse me please	*Vabandage palun*
Help me please	*Aidake, palun*
More slowly please	*Aeglasemalt, palun*

Repeat it please	*Korrake, palun*
Write it down please	*Kirjutage see üles, palun*
I do not understand	*Ma ei saa aru*
I do not want	*Ma ei taha*
It is (too) late	*See on (liiga) hilja*
It is bad	*See on halb*
It is good	*See on hea*
Silence, please	*Vaikust palun*
Wait	*Oodake*

Signs

No parking	*Parkimine keelatud*
Speed limit	*Kiiruspiirang*
Entrance	*Sissepääs*
No entry	*Mitte siseneda*
Exit	*Väljapääs*
Emergency exit	*Tagavaraväljapääs*
Open	*Avatud*
Closed	*Suletud*
Toilet	*WC*

Language

Travelling

Call a taxi, please	*Kutsuge, palun, takso*
Call an ambulance	*Kutsuge kiirabi*
I have lost my way	*Olen eksinud*
My car has broken down	*Mul läks auto katki*
My luggage is missing	*Minu pagas on kadunud*
passport	*pass*
valid visa	*kehtiv viisa*
customs, customs duty	*toll, tollimaks*
baggage room	*pagasiruum*
airport	*lennujaam*
bus stop	*bussipeatus*
coach terminal	*bussijaam*
ferry port	*reisisadam*
railway station	*raudteejaam*
(city) centre	*(kesklinn) keskus*
street, square	*tänav, väljak*
traffic lights	*valgusfoor*
car repair	*autoparandus*
driver's licence	*juhiluba*
traffic accident	*liiklusõnnetus*
traffic police	*liikluspolitseinik*

back	*tagasi*
forward	*edasi*
straight ahead	*otse*
to the east	*ida suunas*
to the left	*vasakule*
to the north	*põhja suunas*
to the right	*paremale*
to the south	*lõuna suunas*
to the west	*lääne suunas*

Money

credit card	*krediitkaart*
currency exchange	*valuutavahetus*
exchange rate	*vahetuskurss*
free of charge	*tasuta*
in cash	*sularahas*

Accommodation

vacant room	*vaba tuba*
with bath (shower)	*vanniga (dushiga)*
with private toilet	*oma tualettruumiga*
at the front	*tänava poole*

Language

at the back	*hoovi poole*
on a lower floor	*madalamal korrusel*
reduction for children	*allahindlus lastele*
an extra bed	*lisavoodi*
hot and cold water	*soe ja külm vesi*
kitchen facilities	*köögi kasutamine*
Is there an elevator?	*Kas teil lift on?*
Please clean this	*Palun see puhastada*
Please wash this	*Palun see pesta*
The voltage is 220	*Elektripinge on 220*

Restaurants and meals

beer	*õlu*
coffee (with milk)	*kohv (piimaga)*
drinking water	*joogivesi*
juice	*mahl*
milk	*piim*
mineral water	*mineraalvesi*
wine (red, white)	*vein (punane, valge)*
wine list	*veinikaart*
Estonian cuisine	*Eesti köök*
beefsteak	*biifsteek*

boiled/oven-baked potatoes	*keedetud/ahjus küpsetatud kartulid*
brown/white bread	*must/valge leib*
fried fish	*praetud kala*
green salad	*roheline salat*
mutton/lamb	*lambaliha/talleliha*
roast chicken	*kanapraad*
roast pork	seapraad
roast turkey	*kalkunipraad*
salt	*sool*
seafood	*mereannid*
sugar	*suhkur*
veal	*loomaliha*
vegetable soup	*köögiviljasupp*
vegetarian dishes	*taimetoidud*

Days

Monday	*esmaspäev*
Tuesday	*teisipäev*
Wednesday	*kolmapäev*
Thursday	*neljapäev*
Friday	*reede*
Saturday	*laupäev*

Language

Sunday	*puhapäev*
today	*täna*
yesterday	*eile*
tomorrow	*homme*

Numbers

1	*üks*	8	*kaheksa*
2	*kaks*	9	*üheksa*
3	*kolm*	10	*kümme*
4	*neli*	11	*üksteist*
5	*viis*	12	*kaksteist*
6	*kuus*	20	*kakskümmend*
7	*seitse*	100	*sada*

13

BOOKS

Books published in Tallinn for sale to foreigners, although well produced and well translated, are often disappointing. At one end, they would weigh down even the sturdiest of coffee tables while at the other they are little more than pamphlets. Not much remains in between and it is surprising that there is still not a single guidebook to Tallinn produced there. Most titles available cover just a single building or a single theme. In this latter category two recent publications stand out, *20th Century Architecture in Tallinn* by Karin Hallas and *Walking in Old Tallinn* by Tõnu Koger. The year 2003 saw the Tallinn Tourist Board beginning to publish for the public. Their first four *Curiosity Walks* pamphlets are titled: *Churches, Kadriorg, Lower Town* and *Toompea*. One on Soviet Tallinn is due to follow in 2004.

The Living Past of Tallinn by Elena Rannu, first published in Soviet times, continues to appear and covers the period up to the death of Peter the Great in 1725. It is effective in its portrayal of day-to-day life on the streets. *The History of Old Tallinn* by Raimo Pullat, first published in 1998, is rather ponderous but continues its coverage until the beginning of the Soviet era.

The Estonian Institute produces a wide range of fact sheets and two magazines, *Estonian Art* and *ELM (Estonian Literature Magazine)*. Estonian embassies usually stock these but they are now published in full on the institute's website: www.einst.ee. They are an excellent substitute for books that still need to be published. In Tallinn they can be obtained from the institute's office at Suur Karja 14. They have a refreshing sense of humour (and sense of realism) lacking in so many other Estonian publications. A second Estonian Institute website www.estonica.org offers an encyclopaedia on Estonian topics such as culture, history, nature etc.

The second-hand bookshops still have an extensive stock from the Soviet period. These shops also have a good selection of books on art and sculpture, none of which have been subsequently brought up to date. *Tallinn, A Tourist Guidebook* by H Taliste appeared in many editions during the 1970s and 1980s as did *A Guidebook to Tallinn* by Raimo Pullat. Both are interesting not only for the photographs of wide empty streets and statues now pulled down but also for their interpretation of Estonian history. Only 10–12 restaurants were listed throughout this time.

No travel books dating from before WWII have been republished since then but copies of *Baltic Corner, Travel in Estonia* by Ronald Seth, published in 1939, can still be found. Several chapters cover Tallinn. The year 2003 fortunately saw a new edition of Arthur Ransome's *Racundra's First Cruise*, edited by Brian Hammett, which commemorates the 80th anniversary of this expedition which took place in 1923. Not only did Ransome include Tallinn and Paldiski in this journey but he also married his second wife Evgenia at the British Consulate in Tallinn in 1924. She had previously worked as Trotsky's secretary in St Petersburg.

MAPS

No decent maps of Tallinn or Estonia are published outside the country. The main publisher in Tallinn is Regio, whose maps are in all the main bookshops. Foreigners planning to travel around Tallinn usually buy their *Ühistranspordi kaart* (public transport map) and those travelling further afield their *Eesti Teede Atlas* (Estonian Road Atlas). These are updated every year and are available in Britain at Stanfords in London, Bristol and Manchester. Maps and atlases covering the three Baltic states are produced by the Latvian publisher Jana Seta and these are available both in Britain and in Estonia.

WEBSITES

Estonian Institute www.einst.ee, www.estonica.org
Estonian Ministry of Foreign Affairs www.vm.ee
Estonian search engine www.neti.ee
Estonian Tourist Board www.visitestonia.com
Tallinn City Council www.tallinn.ee
Tallinn Tourist Board www.tourism.tallinn.ee

Each of these sites has links to many others with more detailed information. The Estonian Institute should be the first port of call for further background on anything cultural and the MFA for anything political. The Estonian search engine quoted has a very wide database that probably includes everything published in foreign languages in the country as well as covering every Estonian daily and weekly newspaper. It is useful for tracking down information on less well-known people and places.

Pocket an expert!
More mini guides from Bradt

Comprehensive coverage of a range of European cities,
complemented by full-colour street maps.

Budapest Adrian Phillips & Jo Scotchmer
(due September 2004)
With its Parisian boulevards and illuminated bridges, Budapest
is the most romantic of cities. This Bradt guide takes you
from the castle and caves to the shops and spas, and provides
all the practical details you'll need for a great short break.

Cork Linda Fallon *(due November 2004)*
Join the people of Cork as they celebrate their city's status
as European Capital of Culture for 2005. Local writer Linda
Fallon takes the visitor through the festivals, guided tours,
pubs and restaurants, and even sporting events, that have
brought Ireland's second city to prominence.

Dubrovnik Piers Letcher *(due December 2004)*

Piers Letcher brings his in-depth knowledge of Croatia to this historic walled town, fast becoming a popular short-break destination. Here is everything for that idyllic break, from nightlife and the best local restaurants to island retreats and nearby national parks.

Kiev Andrew Evans *(due December 2004)*

Kiev, the birthplace of Slavic culture, is a city sparkling with the golden domes of a hundred churches. Features in this guide by the author of Bradt's guide to Ukraine include city tours, architectural highlights, local transport and – of course – plenty of places to eat and drink.

Coming in 2005 *Riga, Vilnius, Ljubljana*

Available from all good bookshops, or by post, fax, phone or internet direct from:

Bradt Travel Guides Ltd
19 High Street, Chalfont St Peter, Bucks SL9 9QE, England
Tel: +44 1753 893444 Fax: +44 1753 892333
Email: info@bradt-travelguides.com Web: www.bradt-travelguides.com

Index

174

Overview of Tallinn Old Town (TH)

Town Hall Square (JS)

Traditional dancing (TH)

Street scene with Church of the Transfiguration (HB)

Alexander Nevsky Cathedral (HB)

LONDON GATWICK TO
Tallinn

* Every day
* Non stop
* Great fares
* No advance purchase
* No minimum stay

ESTONIAN AIR
www.estonian-air.com

For more information contact your travel
specialist or call us on 020 7333 0196.

2 OLD TOWN

A **B** **C** **D** **E**

1

2

3

4

Energy Museum

Fat Margaret's Tower/ Maritime Museum

RANNAMÄE TEE

MERE PST

Architecture Museum

AHTRI

N

Bradt

PÕHJA PST

Hotel Meriton Old Town

KOTZEBUE

SUURTUKI

Hotel Skåne

KOPLI

RANNAMÄE TEE

TOOMPUIESTEE

Hotel Three Sisters

St Olav's Church

Natural History Museum

Tornide väljak

Applied Arts Museum

SUUR KLOOSTRI

LAI

PIKK

Local bus station

NUNNE

Estonian History Museum

Imperial Hotel

Railway station

Toompark

Snelli tiik

RAHUKOHTU

RATA SKÄEVU

PIKK

St Petersbourg

DUNKRI

KULLASSEPA

map continues page 3

TOWN HALL SQUARE

Town Hall

Photographic Museum

VÄIKE-RANNAVARAV

UUS

VENE

Health Museum

Tallinn City Museum

Park Consul Hotel

Holy Ghost Church

Pharmacy

St Nicholas' Church

AIA

MÜÜRIVAHE

UUS

Dominican Monastery

VENE

VIRU

Taanilinna Hotel

Fire-fighting Museum

Viru Gate

Vana Wiru

Viruvärava mägi

MÜÜRIVAHE

VIRU

Hotel Barons

MERE PST

Central post office

VIRU-VÄLJAK

V Ho

Tamm-saarepark

PÄRNU MNT

i